Audio-Visual Teaching

Audio-Visual Teaching
The Holistic Thinking

Rajni Tandon

SHIPRA

(First Published in India in 2011)

Rs. 895, US$ 30

ISBN: 978-81-7541-513-3

2024 Impression, PoD

Audio-Visual Teaching: The Holistic Thinking

Published by:
SHIPRA PUBLICATIONS
LG 18-19, Pankaj Central Market,
I.P. Ext., Patparganj, Delhi 110092, India
11 47322068, 22235152/6152; 9650028065
info@shiprapublication.com
www.shiprapublication.com

Preface

Life-long learning has become the biggest challenge in our open communicative world order. The threat to survival that surrounds us needs radical changes in educating the vast populaces that are struggling against the constant tensions of co-existence. This book addresses the academic bases that establish some systems for developing content arrays to use digital media for holistic education. Arthur Schopenhauer conceived of the World as Idea and declared that the principle of Sufficient Reason was the ground upon which life-living is executed by persons in Space and Time. The infinite variety of interactive growth through the co-relating of cause and effect needs systemic formats that open thoughts as designs about taking responsibilities. Diverse exercises that cyclically integrate co-related sets of parts to work upon desirable wholes of peaceful harmony become models for progressive interaction.

Audio-visual teaching is a very precise and dramatic exercise in combining reality with possibility in systematic approach towards using pre defined concepts, classical theories, ritual arts for communicating, and artifices for stylizing to combine and compose various skill sets to reveal our applied humanism. The nucleus of our interactively shared applied humanism emanates from total trust in the skills we evolve to make us sufficiently competent to be successful partners.

To know how to deal with difficulties is the subtle art of convincing oneself about the kind of value framework that can solve a type of situated problem. The inspiration behind this book comes from the concept of *Kshetragyana* that has been stated in the thirteenth chapter of the Bhagwat Gita. Sri Krishna exhorts harmony of thought to battle with the evil that humans can spread.

There were legions of thinkers whose works have stimulated and sustained me and I am deeply indebted to all of them. A select bibliography of some other proponents of holistic thinking that guided me is attached. Foremost among the living great humanist thinkers who have inspired me is Dr Karan Singh. I would not be wrong in saying that he has helped an entire generation in being steadfastly loyal to each ones Religion.

This book can help teachers to give free reign to their imagination while guiding students of any age or clime.

CONTENTS

Chapter One

Audio-Visual Languages and Holistic Academics

Human actors use their intelligence to build all kinds of connections between live and inanimate environments to mutate matter and produce many kinds of consumable goods for sustaining different forms of life. The ever changing reality of Nature creates compulsive pressures to form movements, which, in human beings become challenges for maintaining life. Diverse atomic energies within us need sustenance to create benefits and be benevolent to manage the living as spans of creative co-existence. We function to serve the needs of maintaining life in all its diversity by working with each other to produce goods and spread happiness through numerous kinds of evaluated decisions to act and react. Our thoughts are ever emerging designs of logic that get stored as categories of understanding to be used as resources for performing our roles with all the expertise that we can muster. Will power is a marvellous, unique and fascinating gift of creative energy that makes us, ever thinking humans, derive and devise strategies to form, frame, and redirect the information that we have absorbed to display our applied humanity. Each interactive encounter has a hidden energy potential for effecting some growth through our choices for doing some kind of good work.

Audio-visual communication illustrates how we are always "doers" committing ourselves to undertake "deeds" by remaining within a "domain" of execution to "serve" some "purpose" that is reasoned and planned in "different" ways to suit various kinds of partnerships. All actions are holistic in themselves as they are circuits for stimulating each other and getting responses to deal with some aspect of on going existence. An encounter with others and the environment has a foreground movement that is placed within a backdrop for engagement. A life is given to a situation which is bound by conditions and states to pursue an aim in time, and to make our presence felt. Motives build intentions which result in different aims for reducing some of the endless problems that keep emerging. Our movements fit into backgrounds of previous happenings and flow ahead by confronting some difficulty to attain some gain. The notion of playing a part as a portion in a relationship is always present as humans strive to make their presence felt. We keep reinventing desires and cope with the difficulties that arise only by being sure of a system for tackling them. Conditions in the environment need to be understood before selecting multi-disciplinary frameworks of contents which can inclusively examine, expose, explain, explore, and expand sets of growth.

Filmed reality is a complex network of divisions that present sets of orders to manage the fellowships that sustain psycho-civilization. Holism lies in suggesting new directions to make good use of human curiosity which is the sap of the spirit that keeps urging us to work to open some benefit despite facing many difficulties. At the focal centre of divulging information is the multipurpose, many levelled spread of images that are vibrant, radiant and colourful representations to illuminate our capacity for "seeing" and charging or changing our ambitions. A sense of movement made as different motions to make the right moves is the way real life is captured by the images chosen to mirror life-in-as-interaction. The essence of being a strong, sensible and caring person lies in being creative in competent ways of using the skills we acquire.

Human dealings are made up of multiple tasks that flow together but have separate passageways that are discrete components for composite execution. Perception is therefore set into co-related images to design units of wide and deep thinking about 'Me and We' to be worked out as inputs from 'I and You' to provide outputs of consumption for 'They and Them'. Information about how this social validation opens up some processes as procedures to be followed as patterns of progress. Scenes of actual interaction work within scenarios of ongoing labour to merge into different ways of upholding certain causes to establish good growth for others. The open participative dynamic of dialogue indicates orders for life-long learning by sensing wholeness and propulsion as operative functions whereby persons enter into positions to render some applied venture made up of deals and deeds of different types of dealings. Conventions and norms help us to make entries and exits at suitable moments to manage our role taking obligations.

An audio-visual unit presents a range of interactive circuits as parts to be played to form paths to make persons perform as effective partners developing some types of benefits. Each situated encounter has its own importance and needs to be given total attention. We can be givers at one moment and takers in another. Designs for living become supreme goals. Our responsibilities as partners make us innovate to produce and deliver goods for common consumption. We keep noting how we can give our share to serve life by contributing to some politically sponsored frameworks of orderly growth. Collectives need supplies for physical survival, information for the mind, satisfaction for the emotions and opportunities to learn, work and earn. Many types of benefactors are needed to continuously create benefits to help sets of beneficiaries. Learning how to teach through the audio-visual mode is all about getting people involved in making very practical and sensitively perceived choices for fulfilling given and taken roles. Although we work for others we expect some gain for ourselves. There are many subtle ways in which visual truths open great critical awareness about each others' limitations and strengths.

Multimedia languages mirror reality to reveal how persons study conditions and gather data which is mapped to fit into forms for executing different areas of work. An encyclopaedic accumulation of the variety and diversity of existence needs a circular pattern of control to bind and bond certain types of information. We learn to scan images to interpret some conditions to infer ways of building interactions during different sets of encounters. A lot of analysis and synthesis reveals the tasks to be taken to function by implementing some objectives to nurture growth. Electronic communication brings into the open the subtle ways in which thoughts arise as reiterative patterns of conviction to make humans act/respond to needs, desires and conditions. All kinds of gestural, non-formal and formal languages become resource bases for learning to excel as we freely share suggestions about forming the reality that concerns life in the world we inhabit.

Education has to be restructured to suit the existing and different types of systems which enable the spread of designs for living. Teaching through the audio-visual mode reverses the traditional fact based definitiveness that is theoretically validated to open realistic designs for processing new possibilities for better private/public progress. The "subject" in a digital presentation is a type of task planning labour that needs verbs of "activation" to satisfy "product-making" in accordance with skilled abilities. The need to practice upon the choices made from the theories that are available for our use is a constant search. Sets of typical situated encounters become focal themes which are differentiated into sets of components. Both features of significant and conditioned realities affect the progress linked with the awareness of human interactivities. Subtle details with facts to develop impressive dialogues to make like better or worse.

All kinds of divisions and variations, differences and unifications qualities and quantities impinge upon the flows within which life exists. The access we have to the facilities that help us to fulfil our obligations towards those who have expectations from us, the applications that emanate from the habits and attitudes that have governed our thoughts, the experiences that we have acquired by interacting with others, the factors that limit our progress in the environment around us and the enthusiastic response that we can give to certain kinds of stimulation are the variables that need strong dosages of holistic awareness. An innate fascination for attractive form is an undercurrent behind the sensitivity of sincere love which is to be revealed through our concern for others. Conduct becomes very important as we confront environments by learning to think and increase our capacities and skills for processing the joint partnerships through which we nurture life.

We need to begin the journey into holistic audio-visual materials development by trying to understand what being human is and what it can be. There is a constant drama at play deep within the conscious awareness we have for working in diverse ways to contain, control and communicate our inner trusts while converting felt ideas into items to satisfy important human needs and concerns. George Bernard Shaw said that everything stated is as good as it is dramatic. Drama is a sensibility that comes from a deep sensitivity regarding the inner nature of outward expressions. The sense of the dramatic irony emanates from the inherent duality of the mind that has to choose between the ever flitting Psyche and the steadfast reasoning ordained by Logos. Paths that can structure good growth are full of constant blockages so our privately determined impetus has to be steadily and carefully worked out before we convert it into information. Conflicts and differences, confusions and complexities, difficulties and delays, ambitions and ineptitudes are some common problems that we have to keep confronting us as we select the expressions that make us share our identities. We need to accept that conflicting opinions held by others are realities that cannot be wished away but have to be accosted, appeased and gradually reduced.

Information management about leading a life relies upon all sorts of specially designed expressions to enter into the situations that we accost. A sharp observation is a prerequisite for developing a sense of holism while forming frameworks for framing our experience of world as sequences of operational integrations in order to manage the differences, diversities and divisions of existence. We gather data, scan it and improvise standpoints to process socially valid orders to satisfy some aims related to the objectives of self directed interactive growth. Reasons can be visible and concrete or invisible and vaguely suggestive triggers to devise a better life for others and oneself.

Messages about various types of routines for different kinds of functional operations have to be sent out constantly to refresh the memory about doing things in right ways. We privately map notions before publicly merging them into the relationships that conjointly form reality. Our contributions to develop the way forward are value additions to seek better futures. We have to be confident as we independently equip ourselves by depending upon authentic knowledge to enter into streams of joint ventures which give us name and fame. Since we have to make choices we need to look upon life as drama of the self confronting the role-sets it has to play. The ways in which we play roles productively to live honourably become plausible when we probe into different types of parts and wholes as portions and competencies for being precise about our contributions to sets of joint partnerships. The virtual reality of the audio-visual media challenges us to focus upon situated realities as objects which gather knowledge unto themselves.

The digital mode of audio-visual communication is made up of a comprehensive main frame format that works out co-related slots of perceptive action in many sub systems to concurrently draw attention to the fields and ranges of connections that express our concerns for others in efficient and effective ways. We select themes and develop bundles of referential contents to project the tasks that can enact some work orders as sets of inputs to get some desirable outputs. Meaning chains are instructions that are illustrated images for depicting how some consumable products are experientially created through various modes and systematic methods of labour. Analysis and synthesis are both captured as holistic modules to model work-in-progress. From the gathering of materials to be used to the providing of required tools and the arranging of facilities for giving suitable training to work-forces a digital design also looks into the financing and utilising of a product. Notions of equity, fair play and regulatory controls are also built into the practices for sharing gains. The focal thrust in human resource building education lies in showing how knowledge emancipates when it is reworked with a passionate commitment to manage existential interdependence.

The converting of information into pathways for friendly and considerate life management has to be a tour into different disciplines both as their directive principles and their pragmatic concretizations. Since humans occupy a position in a highway for making strongly felt moves all the discrete design elements become very important. The Humanities that describe patterns of love for each other are like the vehicles, the artistry in the skills that the Arts provide depict the product after working upon the Science of doing things properly. Bundles of wholes help a private person in finding a niche in the public partnership domain of existence. Superlative directions come from the ideals that are espoused by persons as loves to be implicitly obeyed with total dedication. Religiosity is the ultimate code to evaluate life living that religions have projected over the ages to help humans in getting solace by praying to the Power behind the cosmic Universe.

We can now work out a theoretic framework for audio-visually revealing how human presence can be prepared for projecting itself in a free and open world of possibilities. **A system** is the locus for selecting an information base to ensure that our practices can provide basic facilities for satisfying common needs of survival and progress. Meanings are bundles of facts having a placed and time framed identity. The intellect relies upon previews of patterns for playing difficult scenes to fit into complex and compounded scenarios of effort taking. What are the common factors that hold any kind of partnership together?

There are five features that affect human efforts to aspire for progress:

- Working to evolve and sustain an identity by serving a worthy cause,
- Always learning more about sets of matters,
- Getting love and affection and giving it,
- Earning money to live a happy life,
- Respecting the wise counsel of great achievers and following it.

Any, some, or all of these factors provide stimulatory impact. Circuits of meanings should be valid and authentic. Emotional power enhances the facts that are stated about working out some matter. Injunctions about laws for bonding motives into features and binding intentions into tasks are the nuclei for framing atomic energies as chargers for empowering persons to be confident about playing a role. To retrace steps after making errors in judgement is not always possible so we get upset by our carelessness. We learn to be more careful and develop habits of thinking holistically. The big picture is a horizon within which a small effort can be improvised. The chaos and contrariness of a reality is the incentive to take the opportunity to think out now to protect human freedom by noting how some change for the better can be brought about. This reflection can and should be self reflexive so that we can become the models we want others to be.

Digital multimedia tool technologies can process working

relationships of all kinds to develop suitable models of systematically progressive action management for viewers. In our global culture the way we work for common causes while satisfying our personal interests is through very carefully planned partnerships. Contents need to be highlighted as notes along with captions and comments to follow meanings that have dialectic impacts. Oral speech, suggestive sound bytes, mood building backgrounds, and the foreground narration has to be carefully composed to make a strong impact. The pictorial montage should be supported by brief captions to interconnect different types of role making efforts. Descriptions are reports about the ways in which people work as partners within the constraints they face.

Audio-visual designing is multi-creative in terms of scripting inventive interventions from human actors. Any linguistic symbol can be used to show how role-plays are bound by aesthetic, social, civic, legal, political and moral laws of conducting oneself in lifelong overviews. There is always a search for presenting selfhood in harmony building ways of dealing with different situations as encounters by being very elastic about selecting aims to pursue objectives as norms of behaviour. Personally stylised exposition has to be encouraged, enabled, supported and guided to get better results from human inventors. The dialectics of communication is always limited and temporary so the reiteration and accumulation of conceptual notions becomes important. Boredom is the other end of the spectrum that has to be avoided while sending out messages. The search for novelty and utility is the challenge in all kinds of creative communication. While well prepared programs are planned for execution it is the sudden exigency of the issue at stake that impinges upon our delivery of a message.

Electronic technological tools prepare persons for being very effective partners by giving access to resource bases on the internet highways so that our dialogues can be focussed on specific areas of intervention. A concurrent and cyclic reflection about essences opens ever-widening horizons for designing the ways in which we tread pathways to be effective role takers and makers. Search for specific knowledge becomes a click away but the importance of the utilisation lies in the seriousness of the commitment we have to benefit from each other. Facilities that provide skills to create fellowship dominate the situation centred conditions within which multiple partnerships can emerge to nurture growth. The unique individuality that we have becomes a major factor in being sure about "how" we can do "what" for others.

A digital spread is a grand system encompassing many visible and intangible narratives about functioning as partners. A power point presentation is the first promotional unit that "empowers" by navigating between systems for using different kinds of resources to satisfy some basic life managing requirements. Clients who use what is proposed become the primary target receivers. After stating the demand/supply chain the process is stated. Themes are chosen to project the complementary nature of growth. Assorted narratives are scripted as parts and portions that can develop holistic all round growth. Goals are divided into different procedures and patterns to obtain the objectives that can be established. Very precise details of work have to planned and accepted at all levels and stages of interdependent growth. Digital intervention is presented as tightly choreographed scenarios where scenes and sequences for rendering some service to each other are enacted. In order to explore, enhance and enrich human free will the displaying of interaction is voluntary not authoritative. Therefore, as far as possible, themes need to be set as tasks that can be taken to transform vast, wide-ranging and deep perceptions into situation-centred actions.

Audio-visual studies are structured as proposals based upon authentic reports about the features and factors that give rise to legitimate demands and requests of groups of persons. Clarity about work skills precedes the allocations to be given to team members. We need to uphold certain loyalties as we work upon possibilities for growth. Conventions alter the decoding which has to be recoded in fresh interpretations of reality building. An episode limits the imagination to the ambiances of specific role making conversational ambivalences. Team building is essential for performing effectively in the open participative digital design that epitomises a mini world where co-workers having different competencies must control their imagination to serve a consensually accepted goal for building a model unit of inclusive understanding.

Multiple partnerships exist in the global world order. From demands within families to the needs of residents in localities, from the trusts built by regional cultures to the policies of nation states that govern all persons, the collectives inhabiting global village numerous systems of order and control are continually being up-dated as sets of facilities having specific rules and discrete regulations. Team work reduces conflicts and opens new visions and versions of inter-linkages that allow people to work in unison by using their individually unique skill sets.

Academic humanism in a professionally organised digitally driven world is a thorough search about a portion of living life by locating strategies for playing roles in partnerships to frame reality as a continuum of revitalizing processes to maintain civilization. Spreadsheets of researched information need to be placed into cyclically revealed circular patterns of reinforcement about variable options and fixed choices to act in objective goal seeking ways. Parameters are pre drawn to delve into some problems affecting life and living. The locus of conditions has to be tackled by giving instructions in considerate ways to deal with human pride. Target receivers are mathematically quantified to signify the technical qualifications that help us to make some points as pointers for enacting desirable actions in place and time. The inclusive patterns in a digital unit also have to show how we can be reasonable and fair, true and sincere, clever and competent in using our skills to manage the different types of partnerships that compose the contents-as-situated-sites to contain learning to live. Enormous wisdom is needed. Wise thinking has been presented by great wise Gurus over the ages in numerous ways. Vedanta, or the last word in living the good life tells us to locate five divisions to process co-existence. These are: firstly, the fundamental elements forming a whole sphere of intervention; secondly the noting of facts and their associated features; thirdly the cultivated skill building in using tools, fourthly the strategies that are devised to implement a plan from start to finish, in the fifth place, are the historical, scientific and cultural factors that encapsulate working procedures. Fresh enthusiasm for arousing feelings by following fashioned models is the motivating energy for affecting practical fellowship building.

The work to be done to uphold some cause takes the centre-stage. The cause dictates the purposes and finds its own elements and decorations of style to compose the slots of co-relating notions to motivate ingenuity and get satisfaction. Methods have to be clarified, tools have to be provided, supervision has to be rigidly carried out, training has to be facilitated and incentives have to be put in place to get large ventures going. Despite detailed management of steps for different stages and phases of guidance

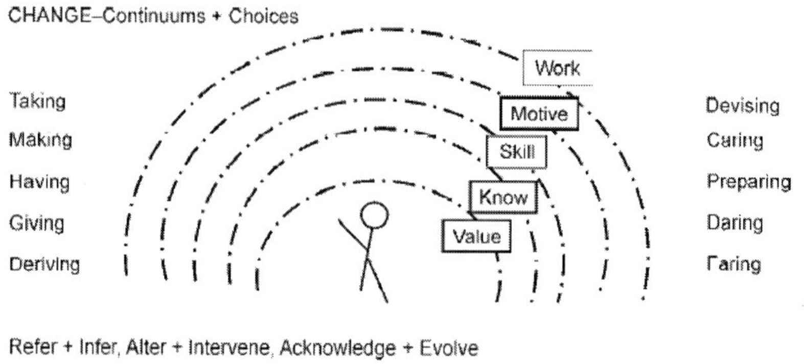

Figure 1.1 shows how we bind dialogues in five sets of value dimensions to motivate interaction.

the actual output remains unpredictable. A professional touch emerges after great practice which also ordains the speed to enhance our efficacy and give the efficiency that comes from certainty.

Perception management is a study not only in thinking about all kinds of parts and wholes of order to manage our strengths and reduce our weaknesses through intellectual wanderings, but also the spiritual energies that work upon bio-genetically given aptitudes. Temperamental vagaries are too powerful and need strong doses of social norms, civil regulations, legal controls and political empowerments to support the moral choices that critically evaluate our evolution. Scenarios are drawn and scenes are displayed to persistently project humanism as constantly serving each other by creating benefits. Many episodes of concrete endeavour affirm notions to be explored and propagated. The reflective principle makes a full circle about "knowing how to do what by mapping why, where and when" to place dialogues in positions. The impact of the message also lies in the best graphic, visual and textual illustrations to expose what is important in precise task oriented ways.

The "full picture" about the ways in which we can enter into the flowing circuits of creative energy reveals task areas for making action-cycles to facilitate the providing of services to share what is needed. We need to build total trust in the universal ideals of togetherness to make moves to "move" into new ways of managing mutual co-existence. Motives dominate intentions and loyalties affect our functions. A sense of routine and creativity simultaneously generate our interventions that must be limited within many types of bonds and boundaries of constraints, convenience and conventions for making co-operative fellowships fructify. Since problems are endless and contentious notions of 'Thou' become the arbiters to decode the ethical postulates to establish significant co-existence.

A radical shift in training teachers is essential because instruction practically exposes gathered data through pictures, voice-texts, and graphic analyses of task taking. Creativity of thought, word, and deed on many levels forms the crux of the scholastic discipline. A deep and wide sense of drama is implicit in the pictured screening together of contents-as-action. A deluge of information dissipates thoughts but a cyclically reiterative expansion of clearly established objectives enhances the memory. It is very important to remember the rhythmic nature of gradual and circular learning. The flow of life works through ever changing demands and we can tackle only some issues at a stage of concentrated endeavour. The rush of energy that makes us enthusiastic and eager to perform does not want any brakes but civil and social mores demand a slower and surer approach. Reason becomes more believable when it is couched in rhyme and rhythm. We can pick up from where we left to continue an adventure as the patient and calm revision gives more efficient and correct strength to our pursuit. Foreground notions of importance are contrasted and compared with backgrounds of real conditions and both types of understanding mix and merge to flow as interrelated actions set in time, place and effort.

The self disciplining quest is set in a project mode to work upon inter-intra human fellowships that can extend goals of viable growth. A lot of permutations and combinations have to be imagined as actual utilizations on the ground by target receivers. Clear definitions, realistic hopes, probable results, logical assumptions and ethical postulates are some factors that give persons the confidence to be creatively pragmatic in their efforts to make progress. Structures need to be presented in stages of actions that are closely interlinked with situations on the ground. The reducing of factions is a major to be tackled in the conversational mode of teaching. The goal is to help persons in discovering better ways of understanding each other while striving to manage the ever emerging problems of survival.

Digital units are made after studying how to present interactive programs by gathering data, researching into textual materials to enhance the impact that will result from the work that is undertaken. Many arrays of contents are collected to clarify the values that can emanate from the project. Role-plays are simulated as actual events to suggest the various responsibilities that accrue from them. Alternate paths are opened so that choice making can be exercised in effective ways. Digital guidance moves between ambivalences about motives and meanings by exposing responsibilities, through stories, comments, illustrations and clarifications so that viewers can be prepared to cope with the confusions, complexities and compounded problems of real cooperative progress. The more persons understand newer approaches to common problems the greater is the ease and speed of role taking. A work culture blends potentials with qualities rather than quantity in making plans.

The free media environment is made up of all kinds of voluminous information that keeps simulating us but our reactions are framed only according to the attractiveness we feel about something, the usability we notice in a message and the result we expect as the outcome of the message. By switching between different types of roles to be played in different conditions, the audio-visual mode makes us realize the drama of accepting different types of situations and failing again and again before getting what we really want. Strife and struggle are like waves in the ocean that batter our consciousness.

An open ended academic approach for managing the partnerships that nurture life picks up texts from everywhere to understand interactive matters in very relevant and precise ways for implementing an effective vision about functioning to suit some specific objectives. Great care is needed to ensure that the multimedia model is emphatically social in equitable ways while being life affirmative, skill based and production oriented. Issues regarding common concerns are designed to uphold ethical principles of equity, justice and an abiding concern for protecting human rights. While disparity is to be reduced differences are honoured as dynamic human actors keep redefining their concern for freedom as responsibility.

The timeliness in the timing of an appropriate action is another dimension that is very important. Confidence building should be the goal while critically examining possible outcomes. Constant reflection designs better moves while trying to move towards some type of growth. The ego gives the confidence to select a plausible option to play a scene and enter a scenario. While the ego is positive and productive it can also be negative and destructive. Habits of distancing oneself from strong feelings to be more objective about sharing our creativity helps to expand, enlarge, accept and evaluate a more critical understanding about role realization.

Stores of information resourced from the internet have to be scanned not only to suit task taking but also to get adjusted with the ideas that the user's personality dictates. Inclusive thinking about objects is easily gathered as concepts of shapes, sizes, forms and usages can be graphically explained. Subjective values are abstract ideals that are too subtle to be declared. Literature, love of artistic expressions, delicate symbolism, metaphoric and idiomatic statements, and flights of fantasies indicate felt energies. Breaking away from preconceived notions is the hardest goal for audio-visual practitioners.

Story lines need to aesthetically present real life to record scenes where the characters open dialogues based upon their adjudicated inferences. Conversations need to include critical views about the state of some affairs and the quests that show how to get support for enhancing facilities that provide better ways of rendering different types of services for collective progress. An understanding of debating techniques is very helpful in making units of live learning because it can help teachers in readily offering suggestions for resolving all kinds of personal, professional and social dilemmas. New insights about conducting our lives are supplied by the digital formatting of the physical, the materialistic, the ideological and the emotional approaches to identity formation to keep helping the ever learning human activist.

Locales are affected by culturally familiar art forms of expression such as visible artefacts that represent heritages. Behaviour patterns that convey special meanings come from age old rituals and belief systems about the trust we have in a religion that gives us renewed hope to carry on with our principles. Family based conventions and social rituals are so deep rooted that they affect the way we open vistas fro creatively responding to stimulants. An understanding of psychological, ethnic sociological social realities is very important for making action-taking partnerships effective and pleasing. Critical evaluation becomes easier when a focal length is narrowed down into a composite range of ideas. Very often the egoistic ambitiousness of some employed workers needs to be cut and pruned and if this is done privately and gently it prevents a lot of the pain coming from the rejection. While universally valid ideals are easily understood, their implementation is a complicated construct that needs oral/written exposure to patterns that uphold togetherness and establish loyalty. Praying is a convention that gives us strength to rise to new heights of satisfactory relationships of all kinds.

The mundane accounting of expenditures often takes administrative efficiency to guide large ventures but in an open to information world the old fear for authority has little place. Studies in management work upon profiles of practical experience and this model looks at all kinds of issues. Very often it is the tangents that cut across different radials which open situations in better ways. Socio-metric sciences are limited to some small percentage of feedbacks about services and cannot be taken as valid assumptions about making global estimates. Precedence have to be given to human centric ambivalences while educating a trajectory of collateral territory based rules and regularities. The concept of "stake-holding" sounds promising but the real stake is the increased job opportunity and the correct guidance and training to make employees think like their employers. A love for the work seeks pure skills but the force of energy to perform is a universally sought essence of self transcendence. Understanding identity framing patterns as devices for following favourite ideals through evocative ideologies is the abiding culture conditioned scenario for progress.

Holistic thinking goes beyond economic interest to prepare formats that critically explore diverse types of human developmental concerns while organising different slots. We make significant contracts when practical action is mixed with moral and ethical imperatives and merged into aesthetic principles that reinstate the spiritual insights behind powerful sharing communicating. Too much negativity is often used and concluded by sarcastic remarks about the unsuitable ideas that overlook limits of social cohesiveness. This carelessly overemphasised dwelling on defects or defeatist attitudes can be so damaging that no positive note can rectify the harm done. Partnership configurations should therefore make allowances for very human ambitions but with a lot of realistic blockages by the ambitions of others. A very close understanding of human nature becomes a real power point for organising multiparty interests in sharing gains with all workers in equitable ways. Episodes should give detailed instructions about producing various types of goods and welfare services as well as show persons how to deal with the fears and fancies of fellow workers.

It is important for teachers to realize that the systems approach dominates all expression because there is a range of management within which dialogue exists. A basic design about the quality of inputs and the quantity of outputs must be very definitive despite having to be flexible. Modalities for multitasked operations can be graphically listed to remind workers about the complete construct. Details break out as slots to frame analyzed tasks into sequences for cohering efforts into sections of the schemata. Clear instructions, considerate supervision and positive thinking are major strategies for ensuring good relations between different types of works that gel together to form a sub unit. A message about implementing a task has to consider the skills, the stage and the phase of the labour and the competence expected from the task takers. In an audio-visual presentation there are no linear instructions. Graphic designs and colour codes are separate categories in numbered subsets of scripting the format of presentation. Points of reference are placed in some order devised by the director of to bond and bind the free imagination into scripted sets of storylines.

Digitally framed audio-visual units should be package deals that can harness multipurpose instructions in different divisions of ranges and dimensions to be used as core modalities for pursuing essential methods. Designers of projects must know exactly what a client wants before planning the details of creative visions. While an overall design lists constituent elements such as manpower and infrastructure, annual targets and establishments, budgets and provision of various kinds of services the detailed production has to be very precise and complete. Brevity in giving instructions, precision in following specific techniques and concentrated thinking about the principles behind a topic are values to be avidly sought by audio-visual knowledge creators. Much research about ground realities and appropriate welfare requirements for employed staff affects the accounting of costs for a large project.

Many practical exercises establish both instrumental and behavioural skills while working on each sub-segments of the venture. Topics are to be scripted in bits and pieces to cover work circuits. A circular design signifies the different set of responsibilities that are to be undertaken. Alternative are stated so that options are there for people having to choose their own paths to give results. Time consciousness is a non-formal factor of socialization that needs special attention in the contemporary fast moving pace of living. Time frames need great emphasis as they determine the help required for enabling the immediate, the near and the farther aspects of operations. Placed spaces for carrying out work orders in different countries have their distinct systems of administration. Employment structures need to follow prevalent conventions about offering remunerations to enrol various types of workers.

Practical procedures work best when they remain within the clearly known milieus for performing functions. Time and task based contributions need facilities and provisions as a matter of course but workers also need a lot of positive support. Digital projects must strive to improve life by satisfying basic requirements such as opening opportunities for improving wage work facilities. Stimulated reality goes into minute details while touching upon conflicting notions that people have about their value systems. At one level is the expanding of horizons about knowing what is to be done and the other is the condition on the grounds which affect understanding workability and beneficence. The circumstances within which new methods for work are to be created by society through the efforts of technically trained individuals is a visionary exercise set in the project mode of digital thinking. Holism confronts change by charging ahead through stimulated role making.

Strengthening memory spans is a major concern and it is to be sought by using many attractive ways of appealing to different sensibilities. Pictures can make their points by themselves as they live through their own artistic truths. Comments and critiques join explanatory narrations in an easy conversational question-answer pattern to make it possible to encourage self-improvement. New possibility may be fanciful at first but they incite individuals to evolve by creating fresh approaches to common problems. Simple and direct statements can be given importance through visual episodes which are commented upon in serious or casual, exaggerated or light hearted or anecdotal ways.

A digital audio-visual set is like a mini-book whose "chapters" are highlights about concurrent streams of actions. A lot of soft skills can project the realistic ways of executing heavy managerial decisions. Persons do not readily show their ignorance through new ways of learning to think about working upon problems have to be directly stated a long with measures to maintain quality controls. Psychological questionnaires are popular ways of being gently reflexive about personal competence. Memory enhancing vocabularies can be used such as alliteration, flowcharting, jingles and graphics that define new patterns. Mood building background music helps by rhythmically establishing sensory receptivity.

Social niceties such as good manners, respect for different types of cultural traditions, reiterating points in different contexts, summarising key factors, maintaining good humour and being very specific are some standard rhetorical techniques that have to be incorporated in visual terms as chunks for understanding thoughts easily. Levels of skill building to attain efficiency have to be properly gauged and executed at different steps and stages to reinforce confidence building. Over emphasis on the mechanics of acquiring a skill is a piecemeal approach that gives credibility to a small part of the totality that audio-visual communication ought to be. It can be counterproductive as it distracts practitioners from the true goal of holistic aesthetics which govern genuine creativity. Exercise based on genres of communication may differ according to the objectives behind relationships but the strengthening of fellow feelings is common. Consistency searches for self-improvement to enhance all kinds of task taking.

Philosophy must precede education through an audio-visual unit per se as it is the focal centre of audio-visually created teaching. The most radical teaching premise is that one has always to commune with oneself before guiding others. This changes the entire teaching methodology. What is clearly known is that some price has to be paid for each and every deliberated choice of action. Critical evaluation arises from notions of right and wrong for an encounter which becomes a habit for noting controversial, negative, chaotic, superficial and silly aspects of self revelation. A micro processing innovativeness shows how each situation is a pathway that opens some routes and closes others. Emotional cleansing of some kind takes place in the broad materialistic sweep of having to participate in interactive polarities.

The acceptance of a religious belief revitalises trust in giving great performances. The seed force of the soul can evolve our humane applications to transcend our own limitations. Praying helps people to reduce tensions caused by the rigorous holds of ambitious striving and the forceful passions of a personal temperament. The ever-present angst of human existence needs the harmony that holism sustains. Teachers must probe into the impact of personal factors while giving lessons. Teachers have to develop a sixth sense about the signals sent by body languages. Some psychosomatic indicators of anxiety and pressure are normal but when they dominate routine activities special attention has to be provided. Persona centred habits are very complex and can be checked and directed. Personality management skills are to be developed by teacher guides with great sincerity and total objectivity. While some formulae can be applied to frame questionnaires to test aptitude and abilities, there are plenty of hidden undercurrents that need to be addressed. Habits for critical scanning should be formed. The critiques should evaluate the teachers themselves. Competitive games open new horizons and strengthen the instinctive search for excellence.

Positive thinking is a major requirement as the confidence expects results in new strivings to make partnerships more professional. Faith has to be considered as energy derived from the divine creator of the world to make humans strive to achieve new heights of self evolution. The absence of supports curtails voluntary action taking. New options that increase voluntary contributions may seem difficult at first but very soon they become popular. Social approval for different options is a great service that audio-visual media can spread. The focus should be on the disciplining of the self as the act of faith that propels behavioural interactions. Differing viewpoints, denials, misunderstanding inner feelings of irritation have to be addressed, not avoided.

The friendly talk show is a new style for spreading holistic understanding. In a talk show a host introduces the points regarding a theme. Many value-additive notions are gathered from invited experts and the members who form a live audience. Cross-examination reveals better options. The goal is to compose a workable format for managing the paths that can serve specific causes. Many pressures and compulsions converge around the state policies that serve to establish public systems to enable person-centred progress to ensure patterns of localised citizenship. Democratic contributions uphold human dignity while managing complex messages to incite viewers to clarify their own notions. The exercise is to locate fresh ideas about making advances towards the future by solving various kinds of problems. The summarizing of the conversational problem solving leads to getting a consensus about some ranges and dimensions of interactive life organisation.

Computer expertise is a very slow and time consuming process. In a consumer driven social order many sponsors are needed to fund holistic lesson building a lot of very expensive professional help is needed at all levels of production. Apart from ample funding to cover man hours of elaborate thinking to create art work for film making, script writers have to incorporate academically sound holism. The ingenuity of inspired thinking cannot be learnt except through personal experience and very dedicated caring that is spiritual in essence. Stories have to be developed in locally set, family based, and profession centred patterns for dealing with day to day existence. The impact of the story often lies in the brilliant way in which the film becomes literary as well as artistic. Attractive shapes of decor and language mixes such as emblems, symbolic touches and mood music strengthen the power of awareness being conveyed.

Animated lines can perform traditional blackboard tasks. Boxes in flowcharts, circles of integrated ideas, radiating designs of slots merge into whole spheres of ideas. The weaving of patterns as ways of experience as simulated sequences are some techniques from the theatre that are required in an audio-visual unit. Camera angles, the length of the shot, the light effects, the fonts that are used and the styles that are selected by teachers who are familiar with the medium constitute electronic expressions.

Dialects of speech need to follow accents, rhythms and gestures. Locales provide colloquial charm, myths and legends open new juxtapositions to give greater energy to a living demonstration. The harsh realities of the problem ridden world are in themselves the incentives that keep challenging us to seek the order that creates new realities. Animated eagerness, enthusiasm about the work and the follow through of an idea to its inclusive bases should be assiduously sought. Just as thoughts bind us with our flowering consciousness efficient problem managing bonds us with each other.

The quest for seeking success in a dialogue is embedded in mystery as human beings are impulsive. Despite planning and mapping what is to be done the actual communication may be misunderstood or avoided. It is only in the case of scientific data that there is predictability in understanding what is meant. When a thought is reiterated as lived experience it remains in the memory and some traces emerge when recall is required. Frequency and familiarity of interactive happenings are like ritual patterns associated with routines of existence. Memory thrives on emotional associations. If thought deals largely with the mundane accounting of concrete tasks notions of loss and gain become limited but when obligations and expectations are given importance a largeness of vision is attained. Opposing states of hopes and fancies, fears and despair, approval and dislike draw upon deep stores of relating with others and give greater confidence in seeking growth.

When a digital module has to deal with vast multitudes of beneficiaries a lot of data gathering becomes a vital pre-project exercise. Specially trained researchers have to compute population figures, analysts work out man-power inputs, economists work out cost benefit ratios. Financiers arrange funds, policy makers balance findings with the memorandums for understanding that entrepreneurs suggest. Lawyers give legal validity to the services that professional companies agree to provide after "experts" verify documents pertaining to multi-party stake holders. The entire circuit often spans many countries on the globe. Human resource development is an advisory consultative exercise that suggests effective training of the trainers who have to implement certain tasks in time bound task allocations. Many standards are laid out to frame the task taking in very precise, detailed and well planned ways. Despite making allowances for exigencies many unforeseen hurdles show how destiny plays the final card in the implementation of a good cause.

The applicable sociology of intersections between models and their implementation comes from a combination of altruism and materialism with spiritually evoked capacities to enhance expressive skills. All media products have educative powers which can be very negative unless a deliberate inculcation of values brings out positive feelings. Commercial supports are essential but the essence lies in the appeal that goes out to affect the hearts of humans.

Designing the Academic Approach to Actual Practices

Holistic thinking has to become a habit for coping with the expectations people have about satisfying the ambitions they have while performing sets of duties. Welfare activities of many kinds are needed to ensure that interactive growth maintains a valid, positive, honest, harmony building dimensions to get creativity. Inner convictions enhance productivity when partnerships are free and open to change. The more alive explanations are about flows of production, the greater is the empathy that evokes creativity in using skill sets. Ideally audio-visual modules are cybernetic visions about constructing infrastructures to enable a safe and sustainable living for all the inhabitants of the earth. An inclusive vision needs to put in place many smaller units to manage the systematic stages and phases of the large globally collaborative intra-country work systems.

Audio-visual teaching is always a challenge because each bit and byte is an opportunity for coping with the evanescent nature of reality by scripting positive proposals about struggling to evolve. Attitudes control aptitudes and benevolence becomes more desirable when we see the result of our actions without making any excuses for ourselves. Positions as responsibilities, policies that perfect some welfare objectives and ensure their delivery to the deserving need delicate balance between fixed promulgations and make allowances for personality based idiosyncrasies. The teacher works on the talents that persons have to constantly labour to nurture our common humanity with ever increasing skilfully developed passionate determination.

We can easily explain a subject by indicating what the components are, how the objectives of growth have to be served, what the procedural tasks are but the real problem is the moulding of human inclination. Weaknesses such as lack of attention, narrow focal range, poor control over disciplining oneself, strengths that are inadequately developed are some factors which add to the negativity that blocks progress. Guidance that is empathetic and loving, non-judgmental yet critical, deeply caring in sustained ways, supportive as well as instructive, theoretic as well as practical are the keys for establishing good growth. A very strict regime and an intense but controlled approach to passion is essential. It comes by distancing oneself from the reactions thrown by the chaos of contradictory and clashing perceptions. Awareness about unrealistic expectations can be controlled by direct statements. This may be a cruel task but is unavoidable. Placatory signals can reduce the pain of moving up into a new critique to handle growth.

The locating of a desirable state of contentment for rejuvenating harmony of thought-in-action can be visualized only when the fundamental discoveries noted in the sciences, arts and commerce are known to all. These academic pillars establish a strong foundation for the humanness of applied humanism. A circular and cyclically reiterative pattern is followed. Texts are linear asides that accentuate the visually design episodes that are the main models. We therefore need to note the spectrum and then form the areas of design. We state conditions and develop the premises for making radical changes. We give a history of the way policies have been implemented so far and how they had to change to open new directions for developing more efficacious paths. We place the paths as positions held by participants in time framed boundaries of execution. We select the focus for advertising the outreach. We give detailed directions to map a route in the inter-linkages between discreet partnerships. We build up infrastructures to prepare the ground for carrying out the proposed project in stages and phases of regulated work orders.

Vocabularies are sequence of ideas to suggest chains of sentences that cumulatively keep processing sets of options to serve the *situation determined directing of selfhood within different types of co-relationships*. Role-playing is shown as the pursuit of a partnership that deals with core parameters and remains within personal yardsticks. *Checklists* are prepared to combine skill sets for implementing ambits and ambivalences of role playing positions. Division are differentiated as sets of processes and as systematically organized procedures.

The multi-system approach to a situation can be taught to young students by building vocabularies in relation to sets of growth processing terms and conditions. Stories about hero figures, new discoveries, novel ideas, puzzles and games, and the great words of wise thinkers, who have done significant work for humanity; helps achievers to counter the dullness that often blocks energy. Using vivid colours to highlight important points, noting examples that are familiar, being courteous and respecting hierarchies are some modes for holding the attention of viewers. Sentence structures become more like lists and notes, critical observations, tables of details, flow charts and other distinctive entries for progress.

Audiovisual presentations clarify temperamental differences by placing them in larger issues about dealing with problems. Some of these are prioritizing ideas, timing an action, curbing over emotionalism and remaining within placed positions. The competitive spirit in play-ways of learning makes rapid thinking easier. A keen sense of reality, history, social customs, literature, aesthetics, sensibility and novelty aids the sensitivity training that brings personality development for audio-visual teaching. While direct concerns hold attention, it is the fascination for pursuing some activity with brilliance that actually determines what we should be saying to whom, when, why and how. Very often boredom becomes a major deterrent and overrides the sense of worth which results in desperation and futility. The greatest crime a unit of communication can do is to be boring.

Audio-visual academics are hard self disciplines which make selfhood both highly developed as well as curtail it to strengthen growth *per se*. Module making is a commodity that should be democratically open ended to allow for participation by experts and aspiring practitioners. Units need to be updated from time to time to become reliable resources for greater productivity. A successful module is one that can be easily replicated for different linguistic and cultural collectives. Discoveries and the adventure that discoverers describe is a very popular mode for attracting attention. A poetic approach to living one's life needs to be painstakingly explored by audio-visual teachers. The use of popular fashions, folk idioms, contemporary jargons and common sense approaches help receiver groups in inferring effective paths of growth. Radical moves to strive for excellence have to remain within environmental constraints and conditional limitations. The freshness of new growth is a bundle of facts, features and futures regarding a range of knowledge.

Studies in holistic academics are essential for opening democracy as the voluntary pursuit of interactive progress. Skill sets acquired by persons keep changing in many ways to suit the stakes that stake builders open as vocations for contemporary consciousness. New permutations and computations combine to evolve new versions of applied humanism in the rapidly changing arenas of life management.

Chapter Two

Mapping Selfhood to Express Dynamic Growth

To be human is to render some service to growth by using our capabilities for working to process the mutative reality of Existence. Questions always exist and seek replies which become ardent quests to be pursued.

We, human adventurers are curious observers, voracious learners, multi-purpose, many leveled thinkers, big dreamers, elaborate planners and faithful believers always doing some work to help each other. Our thoughts are like bright rays of perception that illuminate our actions. Situations govern the dialogues we share to give gifts to each other. Opposite and alternate positions always exist forcing us to exert our choices. We look at the possibilities that can be activated in some definitive relation to the way the world is managed. Cherished beliefs help us to make sense by being sensitive to the sensations that we receive. Recalls from memory open new stimulating ideas for adding to the partnership we are in or visualize. The aim is always to make attractive appeals for seeking desirable responses about carrying out functions in productive ways.

Satisfactory dealings are composite expressions about

workable parameters for producing benefits. We civilize ourselves in socially validated, lawfully sanctioned and intuitively accepted ways of living with others. The demands and desires persons have need to be adjusted within very practical and detailed situation directing endeavors. Human activists are inundated with images and are free to the extent to which they can make '*sense*' out of them to cope with the real difficulties they encounter. While cognition is scientific and definitive the heart is expansive and kind. The acquiring of skills to be competent in different kinds of languages precedes the ways in which human beings commit themselves to project their concerns. At all times there is a choice to be made between diverse kinds of alternatives, conflicts have to be *overcome* and information that is *incomplete* results in failures while *dealing* with others. Persons learn to *obey many rules* and follow *essential regulations.* Many different individualistic strengths and limitations *have to be accepted* as we enter into partnerships that make us humans civilized care givers.

Routine daily existence is made up of '*roles*' which are socially established constructs both assigned and taken as planned maps for rendering services to the environments within which we exist. A *role* is played according to a personally framed *goal* which is defined by *purpose,* driven by *cause,* and developed according to *sets of reasons* through *acts* that satisfy certain *aims. A task* is the operative performance that serves to satisfy an identified need. *Statements* are based upon reasons and the reality that is familiar to others. *Motives* affect the choices we make to implement our duties and desires by working upon the intentions that we frame to expand progress in types of partnerships.

We prepare our *dialogues and present them* through some chosen languages as meanings that can guide us in performing our functions. *A situated encounter between interacting persons has a life* that is framed by the concerns that make persons locate ideas that can create *effective practices* for establishing better conditions for each other.

Selfhood is consciousness that is latent but becomes dynamic when we apply ourselves to act upon what seems useful, relevant, correct, worthwhile and beautiful in relation to some problem that surrounds us. Knowledge about developing better conditions for each other is the foundation for offering the suggestions we make. A vision of some order is derived by understanding matters enough to locate what we ought to do for upholding some valuable cause while dealing with others. The logic we draw upon to deal with problematic issues needs the intensity generated by feelings to propel us towards making changes while staying within familiar ways of working out some kind of progress. Each intervention we offer takes place in a situation and performs a miniscule service towards implementing a prospective path that leads to the production of some object or experience having value.

Communication is made up of significant themes that gather references to infer what should be said to whom in an objective context of subjective thinking. We compose our thoughts into topics that intermingle as briefs to expose, explain, initiate, constitute and institute interactive life organization. Each expression we offer assumes what different others will want to know and will be able to understand and accept as a logical and valid definition. It is easy to study and build formal and inclusive scripts about conditions as facts and materials as objects but it is much harder to incorporate the sensitivity we have for being considerate about the feelings of others. Giving importance to others has some socio-cultural norms and forms but the inner love we feel is nebulous and needs a lot of ego management. *Role-plays are sets of tasks based upon obligatory relationships* which are voluntarily taken as positions to work for in conjunction with others. The scenario exerts a pressure and although we know a lot, we keep searching for new ways of playing our allocated parts. We keep striving to know what is correct and useful, right and worthwhile, true and beautiful and can be done, should be done and must be done. We hanker for many things and try to attain all that we feel we must have. Our own ambitions keep challenging us to struggle against all kinds of set backs to attain our objectives. We copy others' dream about great dramas for ourselves, make plans about all kinds of gains, talk big to impress others and somehow manage to control the deeply felt emotional disturbances that keep arising as we work with each other. We talk about prospects for making products of common consumption and explore them in detail. Whether hearers listen to us or not is never clear, except through formal agreements about joint activities.

A keen observation of the moods of others should be, and does get incorporated in the tenor of a unit of dialogue. We change the way we say what we mean and this inclusion of empathy is extremely important. Our tones of uttering sentences and our styles of writing have as much impact as the cleverness of the viewpoints that extend growth. Both logical lucidity and loving care for the other is the holistic approach to humane "messaging".

Many silent, internal activities open maps to reveal what we have accepted as being useful, significant, trustworthy and suitable for execution in a specific type of situation.

Concepts about need based sharing should be experientially decorated when we make our statements, requests and answers to resolve different types of problems. The ancient sage Gautama, who revealed the Nyaya theory of logic says that each statement we utter is a "sannidhi", or joining together of some entities to indicate a "kriya", task, that signifies effort and has, "aakanksha" or expectation as a, "lacsana" or symbolic indicative value. By extension a concept is made up of many discrete notions to create a complicated set of interconnected meanings. A "karmakaand" is a systemic ritual about our actions according to certain social norms and linguistic standards about what is proper in a relationship for interacting to enable some kind of progress. The "kshamata", is the ability we have in skillfully converting our thoughts into messages of intervention to spread some benefits that may accrue from them.

Perception building is the fine art of concentrated thinking that can bear the load for opening a road to operate in multi-factual, closely interlinked, simultaneously circumscribed range of action sets. Self realization is a decorative way of performing our duties in concrete ways.

There are certain forms of communicating that we are fascinated with and it is these aptitudes that we need to pursue and practice upon to share our innate notions. Codes of conduct are conventions to control impulsive self realization. Holistic thinking makes persons broad minded enough to ignore small mistakes. Opinions are final choices but viewpoints change according to the milieu and the scenario. Cultures to control our expressions mean many things in many ways but the bottom line is always a sense of propriety in giving equal rights to others and being delicate about our "niceness."

Courtesy and right manners associated with different areas of dialogue have to be respected and given due precedence while opening contents as deals. Specific needs and demands are spread over many differentials and components which make planned growth implementable but the vagaries of humanism make results unpredictable. We give great importance to the right rules of conduct for others but we find it very difficult to observe them ourselves. It is very comforting to drift into over confidence which becomes a self destructive lack of self control. We have many fears and deficiencies which prevent us from playing our parts. Feelings of anger, worrying about our own interests, being careless, lazy and rude are major defects. When it comes to facing our own feelings our confidence recedes. Faith brings self confidence back and we make new efforts to move ahead with fresh determination. While methodical techniques easily develop into new prospects our habitual ways of thinking interfere in our ways of perceiving reality and we don't succeed. Sometimes we are bold and daring, and eager to do new things, and sometimes we are dull, lazy and depressed and therefore give up our ardent wishes to work in new ways. Mood swings are very real factors so we need to cultivate very open and forgiving minds to ignore small defects. Self criticism enters our consciousness obliquely, slowly and subtly but the mistakes of other role takers become apparent quickly.

A wondrous flow of energy keeps pushing us ahead. It also pulls us back as we charge ahead to cope with ever changing states of being. Critical analysis about the different aspects of the equal rights of all concerned should be the prime consideration while entering into and exiting from different types of relationships. The ever changing tenor of life seems very wrong when something bad happens but, strangely, the downswing is actually a great blessing because an upswing will follow. Learning to merge practical techniques with our private creations of thought out interactions is a delicate pedagogy that is resourced through cultural expressions of behavioral traditions. It is vitally important to build up self confidence to get the courage of conviction for coping with chaotic realities, complex issues, contradictory behaviors and other human weaknesses.

Sooner or later we learn to make tough choices and even forgive others for the hurt inflicted upon us. The images we project in our dialogue can calmly and lightly carry an enacted load or make us heavily respond to the burdens of our duties. The importance of confidence building despite the knowledge that all that happens has an ephemeral reality is, in itself, a root force for guiding persons in experimenting with our life force of creative energy. *The pursuit of art in any dedicated way gives satisfaction as it invokes the energy of the spirit to bring a sense of calm control to refresh us.*

How do we contain multiple contents for mass consumption of ever increasing populaces? The principle of the web and its slots governs the exercises that can manage to control information into themes that contain some aspect of human development as working design for taking necessary action. *The digital genre of holistic communication formats slots of effort to construct our role taking in band-spreads of taking positions to operate upon some specific quests related to an area of responsible living.*

In the past mind mapping used to be picked up from literature and by sharply observing the examples set by others. The contemporary multimedia tools and techniques in the openly communicated world use mind mapping techniques in all the content arrays that they present. Brainstorming to map inputs to get outputs is a sea change that is very difficult for "teaching". A lot of multi-tasking needs all the wisdom we can garner to counsel teams of practitioners in all humility to evoke innovative experiential learning. All-round growth works through the binding of notions into justifiable, valid and sincere models about displaying skill developing principles in situation centered ways of being correct and connected. Continuity of effort and complementary of ideologies is just one half of the support giving. Changes in attitudes can make us cheerful and forgiving, eager and helpful, or angry and adamant so mood management becomes an essential practice.

Traditions of heroism enter innocuously into our lives as the difficulties and responsibilities keep piling up in relentless waves of performing very difficult tasks. While the choice of contents is optional some factors are common such as conventions of politeness and decency and a deep awareness of accountability towards the obligations attached to role-playing. To enable persona oriented progress a lot of peace and harmony has to be built into the democratically built mutual search for divulging knowledge. A balanced and proportionate managing of time that is available for distribution between arrays of role responsibilities becomes a good starting point. Codes of conduct are mentioned to secure the self reflected control we need to exert in order to over-power our own defects and get back the courage to persist in seeking what we desire.

A commentary highlights known facts and builds normative conventions for developing a message in a dialogue. Factions and factors are opened without hiding reality. Myths are de-mystified so that their humanizing essence is explained. Deeper levels of personal progress emerge through comparisons and contrasts which the evaluative intellect ordains to enrich our self communicated journeys. Despite the differences of opinions, intricately divided segments and sub sections, difficult technological and technical details, and distractions we have to keep on firmly controlling the tracks we have set up for ourselves. Often real or simulated incidents become life defining just by virtue of the intensity that is audio-visually generated. There is a *poetry in human relationships* that calls for controlling impulses and disciplining emotions. This comes from familiarity with procedures and a keen observation of the feelings of others forming an interactive set of growth through constructive images, excellence in skills and sharing beautiful, good and true experiences.

Digital units cover identity formation both as a microscopic activity and indicate its macroscopic possibilities. Audio-visual mass media technologies mirror all aspects of behavior to compose dialogues about themes as recurring patterns that can give a clearer "picture" for ensuring stable, self sufficient and evolutionary growth. Holistic perceptions serve to reduce over emotional responses as the fine art of living lies in being broad-minded and opening our hearts to sufferings of other human beings.

A cyclic framework is sequential but not linear but it is reiterative and gradually incremental. Possibilities are opened and options are given as pros and cons for exerting choices. There are no definitive certainties just as in real life. The ease of skill gifted competence that we have mastered reassures us about being right about what we do. Communicative skills are exercises in accurately gauging the probable results our suggestions may have on others. *There is a face value that is immediately sensed.* The passing show of all that happens needs a pose of confidence before publicity expressing our ideas about progress. In order to uphold a precious value we learn to make some personal sacrifice. We may have many unrealistic expectations which need to be eradicated by being compelled to look at the truth. *Masses of populaces need to be supplied with very frequent doses of spiritual thinking through great artistic energy to strengthen their own creativity for bringing humans closer to each other.*

There are strange passions that arise from opinions that are opposite to ours and we learn to deal with them impulsively or by thinking and restraining our reactions.

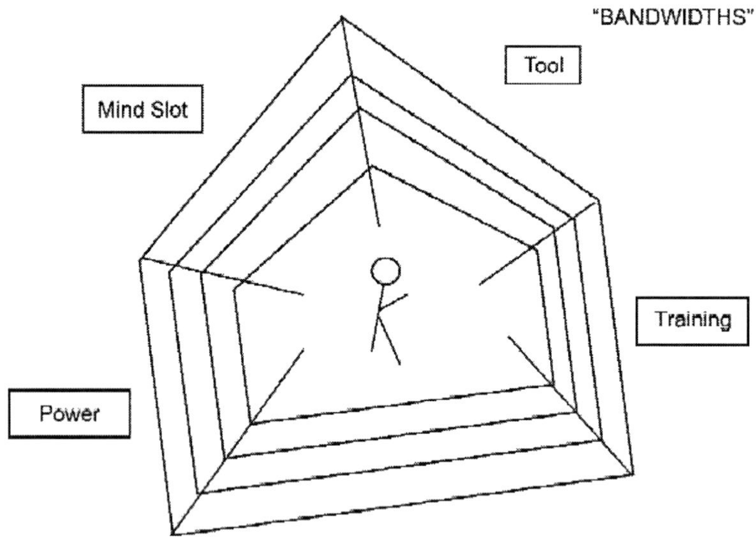

Feel	Hope	- Road	--- Love	--- Bond
Find	Idea	- Goad	--- Know	--- Tend
Fit In	Trust	- Mode	--- Care	--- Trend
Focus	Problem	- Abode	--- Solution	--- Mend
Fix	Task	- Load	— Duty	— Blend

Figure 2.1

HOW WE CONVERT A MIND MAP INTO A REAL ACTION DOMAIN

It is very important to commune with ourselves by recalling what sort of attitude will help in getting our message across with greater power to affect each other.

The first row in Fig. 2.1 indicates emotional pressure. The second goads us with the mental resources we possess. The third row locates the mode along with the mood to convey our impressions and make strong impacts. The fourth row places the conflict in a circuit of reality. The fifth row is our duty to a common goal.

Guidance is elastic and transferable to suit persons having different levels of maturity. We are free to make and follow a well thought out plan and regulate our actions or we can be passionately impulsive or casually relaxed. Life is not "control" based but "contoured" by taking pride in how pleasantly we do nice things. The thrill of perfecting our tasks is to be enjoyed to spread goodwill for other weak human beings everywhere.

Figure 2.2 opens design sets to reveal familiar exercises in venturing to process spheres of interacting as working arrangements that are elastic structures to enable consensus based role realization. A sense of connectedness that is seen in a family is the nexus that opens fresh journeys for working and earning to provide benefits. What life demands from us is an enabling locus for empowering our identity formations. The team guides the temperaments and trusts operate the mutuality factors that we draw upon to suit different ways of relationship building. While types of encounters are the thought spaces sets of factors are the building blocks. Scenes are the services that scenarios of interactivity seek.

Age, experience, comfort levels and frequency of usage are features that affect speech encounters. Dialogues can be

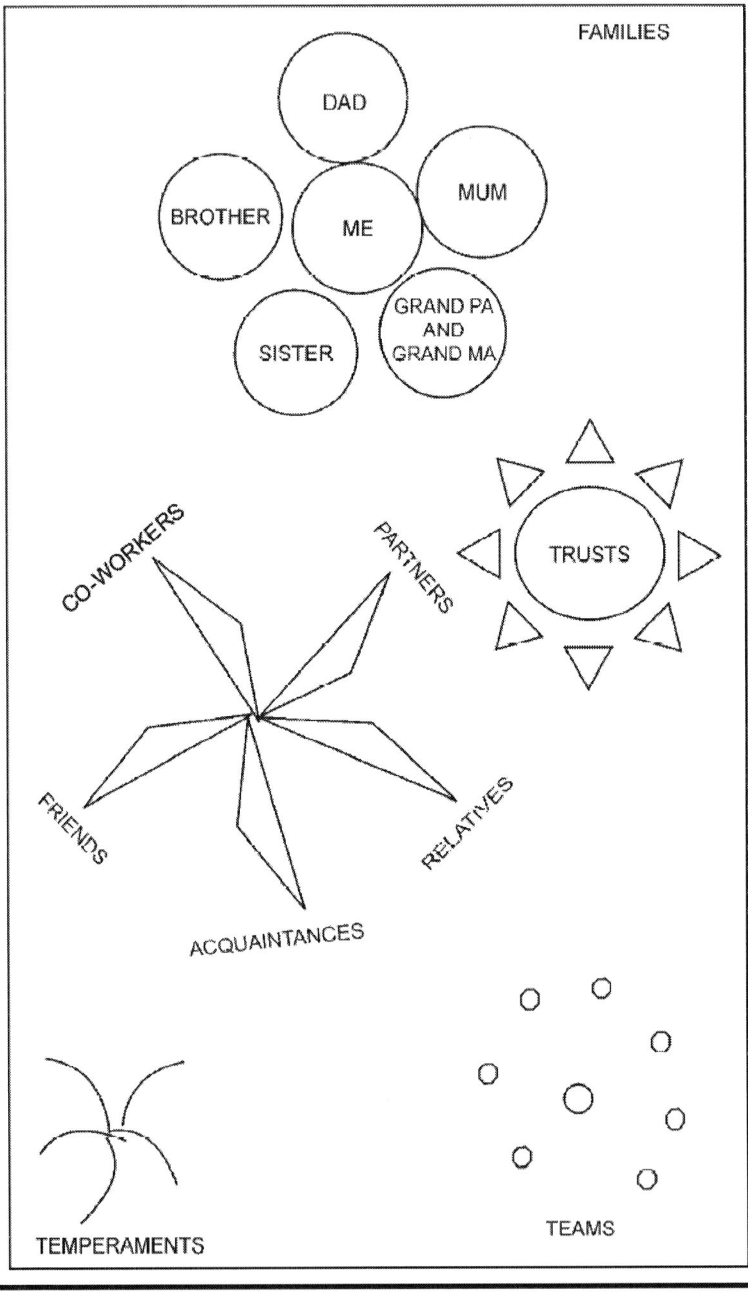
FAMILIES
DAD
BROTHER
ME
MUM
SISTER
GRAND PA
AND
GRAND MA
TRUSTS
CO-WORKERS
PARTNERS
FRIENDS
RELATIVES
ACQUAINTANCES
TEMPERAMENTS
TEAMS

Figure 2.2

supportive and appreciative or drastic and cruel but the clarifying of some positions is essential. A keen perception and quick analysis helps us in reviewing present in terms of the past to clarify a viable future. As we go along alternate possibilities seem to emerge from nowhere and we become more pointed and clever about giving our suggestions. Sensitization comes when we place ourselves in the position held by another and try to reduce the pain of realization. Distancing and involvement are both counterpoints that increase our acumen in gently saying what has to be said.

The mapping of a role as a part in a set space for performing it starts with a check list of tasks to make conversations that propose how to serve certain purposes of functional order. The accountability to the function opens out essential requirements and is subtly connected to an essence of being great. The visual design works upon *Speed and rhythm* in imaging reality. Tonal variations, pitch and accents are acquired in the home from parents and learnt from peers in society. Habits and bio-genetic aptitudes affect enunciation of words as flows in registering dialogue. Oral utterance is a personal pattern that has an impact on the flow of the dialogue. Many movements simultaneously indicated on by the sequential meanings that a story shares. The video camera moves to suit the mood and tenor of the characters. Backdrops are planned according to some speed of thought movements. The foreground is a contrast not only in shades of color and hues of light effects but the movements that symbolize the moves characters make.

Fashions of form and codes of norms condition our dialogues with each other and make us hide our inner feelings by putting on a façade, or transform our secret viewpoints in more creative self realizations. Collective consciousness is made up of regional

Bio-Lingual Revelation

Eyes shine in wonder

Wide face of joy

Energy of concentration

Get dull in boredom

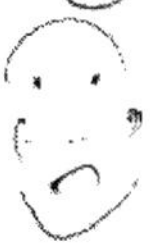

Get small in pain

and local conventions dominates the dialogic designs as use of idioms and faith traditions. Outward appearance such as demeanur, dress, rites for social functions and popular fashions are trusted styles for living in harmony.

The problems of the individuality of temperament and the unity of addressing others' temperaments needs a keen sense of the dramatic and humorous approach along with a sense of loyalty, patience, conviction about what is the truth and the justice in what is said and respect for the very human needs of the persons being addressed. Vivid colors and clever comments attract attention. We identify with raw emotions, appreciate courage, learn to care for what is familiar and pleasant, what is frequently reiterated and what is beautifully expressive and brings out deeper thoughts to make us feel more about core values. Stories about heroic deeds, great discoverers, brave achievers, novel ideas, puzzles and games and the wise words of great teachers fascinate and get immediate attention.

Body languages are unconscious movements that have local, regional and nationality based racial dimensions. These traditional parameters can be indicators of beauty. Smiles light up a face. Eye languages proclaim emotions such as contentment or tension. They shine in wonder and joy brings tears. Sorrow gives a downward droop to facial muscles. Laughter permeates the whole face as it reduces the size of the eyes. Ennui makes us look dull and tragedy brings tears. Gestures of moving in certain ways reflect the postures of thinking in certain ways. Excitement is infectious, anger radiates bad feelings, violence destroys life and calmness contains and controls passions.

Aesthetic designs can subtly open chinks in the facades that mask the tempests of feelings that would deter us from attaining the standards of responsibilities that roles thrust upon us. In this plethora of rules and rulings for self realization it is the deep roots of our conscience which uphold moral ethical values that arbitrate how we making our choices to react/act.

Progress in a global world order is so radical that the logical thinking it portrays needs to be very widespread, precise, wise and very insistent about being effective in implementing the action taken. Howard Gardner has identified ten types of Intelligence. These are cognitive/analytical, bodily/kinesthetic, special/ localized, musical/rhythmic, interpersonal/intrapersonal, natural/ selective, existential/ synthesized, essential/essence based, crafted/aesthetic and having micro value/ macro reference. Digital units build upon some or all of these principles as they deploy duties to define ventures that can adjust with the rapid changes in the world. There are methods for working upon materials by using different tools to make in concrete objects. The likes and dislikes that make us what we are have to be tackled. There are many special abilities and skills that are to be developed to form better habits which can be presented in very creative animations. Special human resource building units are needed to tackle confusions and accept contradictions in order to prepare rural and tribal groups to enlarge their perspectives for entering into the mainstreams of modern civilizations.

Contentious issues need to be controlled through simulated projections that handle complex variables of behavior in managing problems. In a competitive business based world rapidly changing scenarios affect nation wise policy framing with such force to accelerate systems for growth that there is no place left for people to make mistakes or get depressed over failures.

Systematic phases and stages of collaborative interaction are subject to variables of management. Business practices rule the demand and supply principles even in arrangements among families. Skill sets about making efforts in time and place to make significant contributions to flows growth are stated. Team work is the foundation and all co-operators of product development are equal. A spokesperson for the team is democratically elected by consensus. Episodes depict events as chains of links to reveal the necessity of forming sub divisions of implementation. Final drafts are made after a lot of editing at every stage of the venture. Images can be real reconstructed as simulated versions of reality formation.

Financial outlays acquire enormous significance in a sophisticated technology driven world order. The desire to have plenty of money to spend to upon providing resources for nurturing growth even to enter into the information centered market arena creates a lot of pressure and misuse. Digital dialogues need to consider special locality based concessions that do not affect the overall progress of a program to create work wage opportunities.

Linguistic statements need to be set in local parameters. Dialects are collectively given patterns about using vowels and syllables to form sentences. Insistent pressures of hope give hypes to statements. Digital thinking picks up the components of a subject rapidly and notes the procedural tasks along with the problems of holding concentration levels for longer durations. Guidance that is non-judgmental yet critical, supportive while being educative, theoretical as well as practical, and lightly states difficult issues is very important. Boredom is to be strictly avoided along with futility and depression.

The larger the venture the more comprehensive is the designing of roles. Entrepreneurs wanting to open large ventures need proper data collection and drafting of their project proposals. To catch attention the statement of the venture has to open the outputs and the major inputs such as infrastructures and economics, funding and financing, components and tool technologies, numbers of skilled work forces required and work management. Facts and figures about costs and benefits, enablers and facilitators, product deliveries and distribution and the numbers of beneficiaries who will gain have need to be clarified so that presentations can appeal to policy makers.

Many interdependent variables unite to formulate a controlled design by using flow-charts about comprehensively developing the social contracts we have to make by understanding the fields and ranges within which we perform to manage our lives. Legal aid, medical and health needs, civic services, politically supported infrastructural developments are

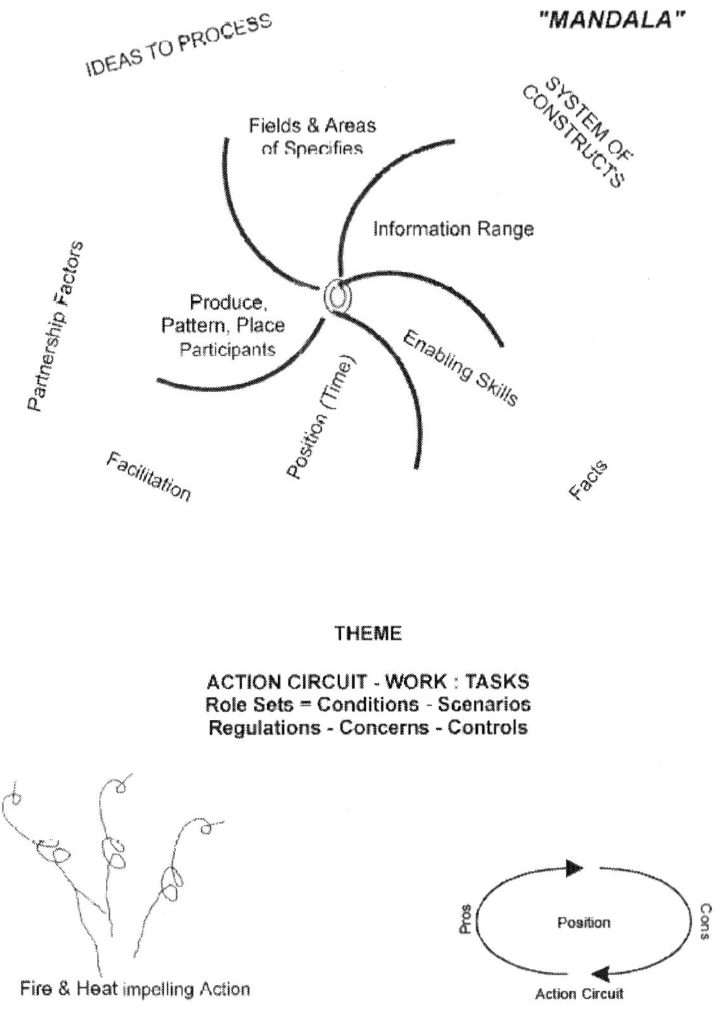

Figure 2.3

some slots that format mutual human co-existence and must enter digital formatting. Time consciousness of demands and supplies is very important for developing a digital proposal. Task allocation and the assessment of work/time co-relations both have a culture and weather based aspect conditioning impact that has to be considered. A comprehensive proposal identifies many sub units that need very careful support structures. Framed filmed sequences illustrate domains of conduct to portray real fragments of participative efforts to suit some field of interaction.

A Mandala is a Pattern about a Set of Deep Inclusive Thinking

An elaborate graphic design de-fragments composite elements to enliven thoughtful attention management for interpreting the larger pictured whole.

Graphic picturing of ideas has a very ancient cultural lineage. Visual meanings enhance and enrich written ideas with a definitive clarity that is realistically valid and can be deeply absorbed. We need to repeatedly focus upon the situation as it is in order to design web pages for inclusively holistic thinking. Role Management is so independent that it needs tremendous educative presentations. Personal states, environmental conditions and motives form three categories that govern our independently chosen reactions and subsequent actions to carry on with the interdependence of living. The flow chart given below opens educative parameters. The first column is dealt with through the last column. In between are the exercise building essentials that apply to the three ranges of developing slots for digital communication. Each sub classification needs to be viewed and reviewed to build a "scenario" for developing a moving scene of responsible action.

Functions	*Objectives*	*Parameters*
reasons	causes	work programs
positions	obligations	responsibilities
practices	social aims	systems of pursuit
regulations	directives	partnership rules
techniques	relationships	theories & paths
Skills	Competence	Arenas

Diverse approaches to common problems, the display of diverse assumptions, questions wanting answers, problems seeking solutions, networking different scenarios in detail and essence are the indexes for preparing powerful models of holistic interactions. Guidance and counseling is a very important area for efficient working. The obsessive nature of passion which leads to aggressiveness is very offensive and workers need to be aware of its dangers. Some psychometric questionnaire based methods help in stress management for all levels of workers.

The quantum and quality of inputs for attaining outputs has to be measured in humane ways of dealing with ever learning dynamic human creators. Super impositions of different ways of thinking can be done to garner multiplicity into private trees denoting interactive intellectual strength.

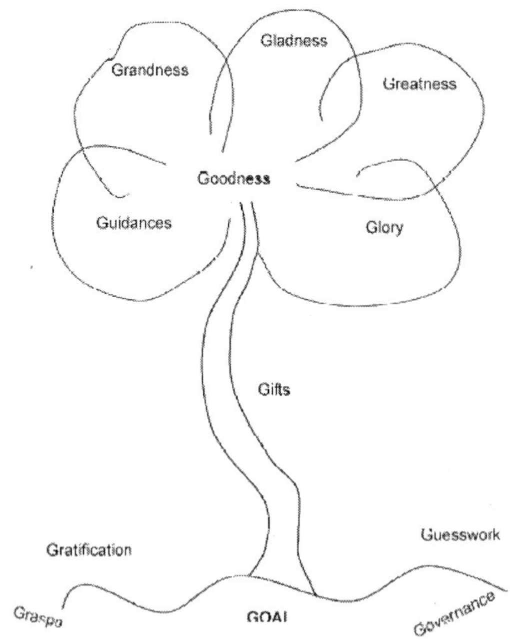

Figure 2.4

- The grand vision and the small detail
- The briefs and the contexts of task taking
- The appeal to the head and to the heart
- The freedom and the dependence of parties
- The value additive designing of technology

Given the constraints and the conflicts that affect human efforts we can benefit from the following exercises: (use as you have formatted)

- Know facts, take chances and estimate impacts
- Box the trust, be honest, loyal and cheerful
- Learn and wonder, seek, struggle and wander

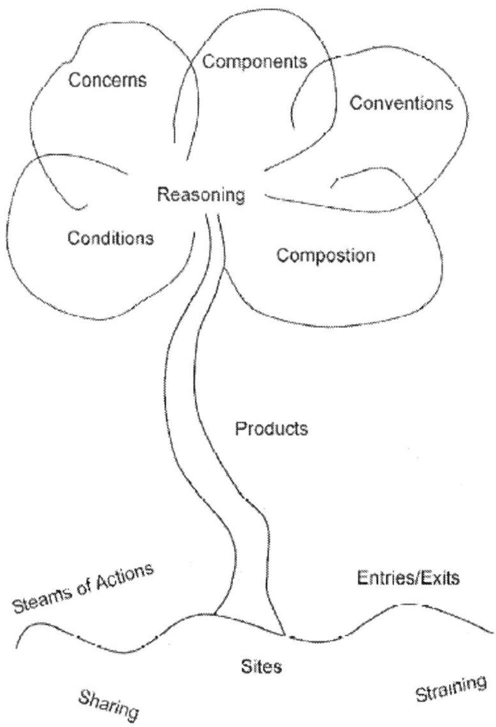

Figure 2.5

- Yearn & earn, spend & be happy & healthy
- Love freely, live lightly & give graciously
- Look carefully, help others & be wise
- Look sharp, feel the drift, heal the rift, give a gift
- Be critical, feel the light, pray to remain right
- Be proper, take the pressure, pay the price & fight
- Be gentle, talk calmly, strive to sight a bright might
- Be clever, share a care, be fair & see spirit sprite
- Look glad, avoid a fad, refine and re define, be fine
- Develop your own style of dealing with others
- Don't hide behind shadows, discover your light
- Don't sulk or show off to hide your hurt ego
- Don't dream without trying to make it real
- Don't be disrespectful even if you feel hatred
- Don't get stuck in a corner, take a turn around it and make an encircling move
- Don't be lonely but be alone to re-examine actions

The mapping of selfhood is a fascinating game played in the inner recesses of our being. We need to be open to destiny by accepting the given life as a manifestation of the Divine Spirit that has created all life. A globally endangered world must uncover our secrets and teach us to revel in our very own humane love for living by tending each positive trace of deeply thought out interaction.

Let us dwell on bio-lingual revelations to enjoy the selfhood that we must keep mapping.

Chapter Three

Applied Knowledge to Develop Digital Lessons

Human nature is a conglomerate of volatile forces that process what we perceive, know, need, want and will in sweeping waves of understanding and reformulation. We are highly gifted in being able to use our thoughts to make transitions from some states of being into others and therein work to serve the causes that can give us a better existence. Actions are intelligently co-related experiments with thoughts that are possible within specific conditions. We can scan many different fields, ranges and formulations of thoughts as flashes to understand ideas in minute milliseconds of time. Our uniquely distinctive intelligence co-relates actions with the ideas that could serve some of the needs and desires that keep emerging.

Thought is a tripartite merging of the value systems we use to understand the facts that surround a range of conditions by considering the factors that affect the growth that can be made in a situated set of interaction. We are guided by the trusts we have in various kinds of beliefs. Our expressions are mentally planned and emotionally executed as pressurized pulls and pushes for making the exchanges that lead to growth. We yearn and we learn to earn name and fame in all kinds of ways and suffer a lot of pain but we carry on doing what seems important for us. An innate sub structuring power manages ever emerging attractions by logically thinking about our positions and environments, our capabilities and competencies as we make assumptions to cope with our concerns.

The volatile ego can seek freedom in all kinds of directions but socially organized conventions force us to reflect and make suitable and more effective choices. We strengthen intellectual energies as we learn to reject the impulses that block our identity formation. The pursuit of wisdom and well being in playing our roles in life is the vast field within which digital guidance is to be formed and framed. At all times there is some kind of tension in our interactions which affects even the ways in which we please ourselves. Dialogues are creative patterns for dealing with various types of difficulties and conflicts, problems and defects, issues and events, differences and divisions as we struggle to become better persons.

Knowledge is applied to substantiate growth in physical efforts by re generating emotional energy to lengthen and strengthen the power of willed intelligence. We are fascinated by operative instructions about making things that work if we follow some conventions to work upon the different fields and dimensions of open participative work.

Consciously deliberated thinking is an eclectic energy that forms visions about growth and selects its own languages to take the opportunity to play a role a situated encounter to join the on-going functions of growth being carried out. Holistic thinking is a study in building perspectives about greater and more valuable understanding about certain matters.

A lesson works through certain categories of activities as

composite dealings made up of some components, provisions and procedures, teamwork and task taking. The will-power to maintain and sustain orderly ways of social and personal progress recycles perceptions as parts to rebuild all kinds of meaningful wholes out of what it knows.

A digital experience is a self reflective study about functioning to supply the demands of living. We knit together all types of useful provisions to work out some kind of benefit and share it to soothe the troubled soul spirit which hankers for satisfactions. The tiny details of togetherness bring about a soothing sense of order and audio-visual messages can provide it. We must learn to examine a lot, experiment a lot, and express our ever expanding reappearing thoughts.

A practical choice is a penetrating ray of *perception* that lights up existence in different ranges and dimensions of systems to manage living among ever changing realities. We give *attention* which is an innate ray of light that illuminates what we see and converts it into what we know in a passing shade of decision making. *Contents* need to give contentment as they open a holistic approach to life by being significant and relevant, attractive and efficient, desirable and beautiful to clarify what should know about a state of existing. *A task that is suggested* has a life within a placed and time bound span of work to fulfill a duty by doing what is proper and expected from us. *Intention* is a motivated decision about joining an on-going activity or creating one that arises from deep within to make us share what we value and trust as being growth productive. Digital teaching helps people to make their presence felt as clever, caring and wise humans who can make sacrifices to get what is important for others and themselves

The tree of *Purpose has a trunk* that predicts the ways in

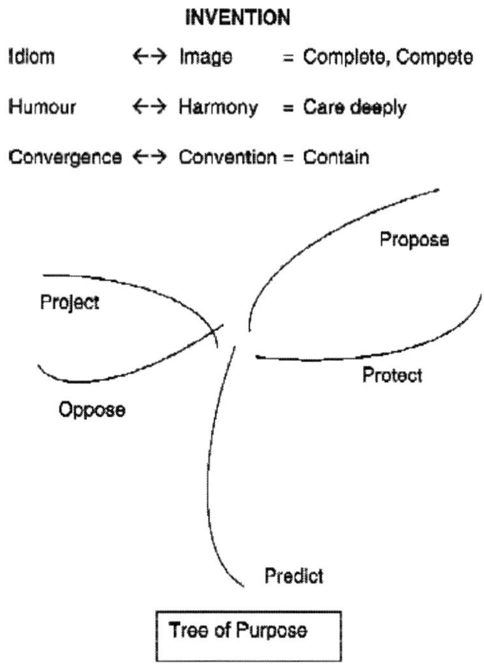

Figure 3.1

which flowers of invention can become interventions to feed life. We *propose* to *protect* and we *oppose* to *project* cycles of suppositions. Our moves recommend as they mend the wounds that they inflict upon each other. Digital spreads open themes by ascribing images to help viewers take the right course by matching experiences with ideologies that converge to open better ways of performing our roles. The aesthetics of making points and counter arguments is the drama of eliciting personal success to carve our paths in accordance with the bio-genetically given gifts that we are blessed with. There is always some tension in our interactions which affects even the ways in which we please ourselves. Communication is a fine art of noting minute details and having enough dedication to take an insult if it will help in establishing a good cause.

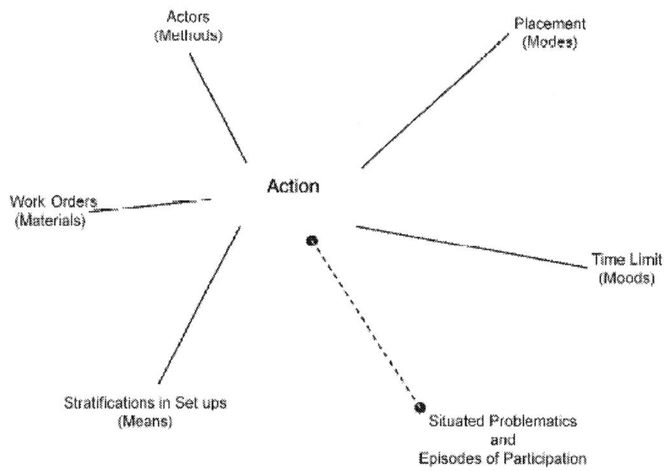

Figure 3.2

In this figure the centre point of action is encased in different points of focal attention which transfers intent to construct. *The dashes between two points are the images about roles to be taken in a bandwidth of accountability for processing given responsibilities.* If we distance ourselves from two points of mental movement and consider the spectrums of systems as categories bound by time, placement and obligations within which we function we get a clearer picture of how we need to allocate our task taking. Materials and facilities are pre arranged set ups that are to be operated upon as strategic labor. Communicative skills which make us bond together thrive upon the partnerships to resolve the oppositions that always exist. We make strategies to connect cause with purpose and adjudicate between the expectations that others have from us and our own patterns of logic to open the conversational choices we make during business like approaches to situated encounters. Endless problems keep emerging and we sort them by finding reasons to make moves according to a range made up of relevance, importance, propriety and priority.

We appreciate the inclusiveness of information about methods and rules to plan further usages by choosing how to react to the given suggestions in our own way of rendering service to the business of living a good life. We learn to develop our own styles for conversing with others about the contents according to our evaluations. Our commitment also depends upon the amount of attention we give to the live digital unit.

Personhood is a very sensitive and fragile picture that we form about ourselves and it spreads subtle rays of awareness that can be noted as characteristics by others. Each encounter with others is encapsulated in a unique environment within which an external shape and form is given to internally decided dialogue to work. We experience a lot of confusions, conflicts, complexities as we are pressurized to find orders, resolutions, and regulations to express the concerns we have for each other. A spirit of ingenuity challenges an existing state of being and overrides the habits that we have acquired. At every step difficulties, mental blocks, rigid ideas, conflicts of interest, negative feelings and contradictory body languages need to be resolved. Creativity and sense of equity, justice behind the search for harmony, love of service and beauty of expression are basic human rights of acquisition and expression that are continuously being derived, framed and formed. Let us review the ways in which we have an effect upon others:

- We are stimulated by sights and sounds, heat and light, colors and composition, smells and flavors, space and shape, weight and texture, properties and productivity and health, wealth and happiness. Visual graphic models explore this faculty to arouse powerful learning experiences.
- Clusters of ideas are expressed in bundles of co-related

dialogues to address different problems. Feelings empower ideas so the more we take our responsibilities seriously the sooner we discover what is effective in a situated encounter. We avidly chase information to find ways of understanding how to build better relationships to deal with conflicts and find a harmonious growth centered way of progress. Real life sequences or simulated presentations expand this sensibility.

- A vibrant pulsating vivid dynamic of interaction comes from knowing different kinds of formed languages and observing non-formal body languages. A strong sense of proportion motivates persons about building harmonious circuits of intent to join various type set scenarios for performing given and taken roles. We repeat or reject what others have taught and said depending upon how we feel about their value in managing an action routine. This delicate and subtle notion building sensitivity has to be affectionately explored.
- The greatest blessing is the capacity to think purposefully about a definitive range and scope of placed and time framed action. We over-ride our tensions when we try to notice the larger picture and locate a more inclusive dimension to our ways of coping with the pressures of routine reality formation. This value accepted adjudicative encoding of interactive functioning has to fit into the flitting and fleeting flows of deciding how to act. It therefore needs to be decoded through very positive visual images about great efforts at securing longer lasting growth.

Digital arrays restrict themselves to situations where functions can be operated by considering important facts for dealing with them. To map a tree for inclusive thinking many

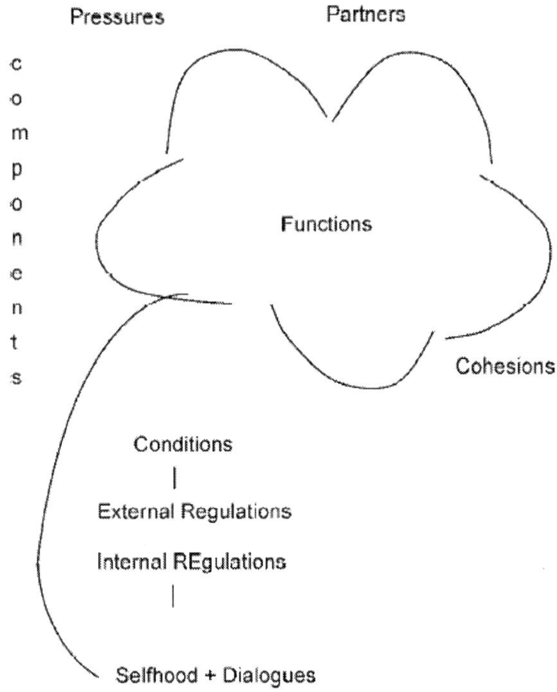

Figure 3.3

references are collected to make inferences about functional value centered interaction. Certain causes are placed into working systems to co-relate reasons and frame detailed designs of task taking. Insights into currently operating techniques make us more creative thinkers. Systems of orderly control are personal as well as publically sociological conventions for managing the care centered controls for being humane.

Experiential knowledge is set into a branched out mapping of many structures. Any system can be moved anywhere as a block of comprehension. A system can be read horizontally or vertically to suit the accumulations that different readers want to locate. Each system stands by itself and can be combined within larger systems to freely explore the arts and skills of guiding each other about the layers of inter-intra action that are projected in the module.

- There are all kinds of systems which build our identities and we often get lost in some of them and close ourselves to others. In an oral dialogue a situated encounter can carry only a small load of specifically stated opinions. Larger objectives are framed as projects that have to be provided for in all ways. The larger and more complex the system that governs us, the more methodical and compounded are the stages and phases for implementing it.
- A system has a format, a history, a life and conveys some instructions about following some regulations to attain stated objectives.
- Systems gather quantities and lay down qualifying measures that depend upon personal value judgments to make responsible contributions to the flows of enabling structures that satisfy some of our needs.
- Multiple Systems are knitted together as inner values and outer functions. Directives and directions arising from the deliberations and experiences of other practitioners that are available to us are included in the slots of the guidance being transferred to others.

The gradual and additive realization of deeper truths is like the bursting of energy that comes from some mysterious charges in the mind. We can gather the energy in a system and store it for later usage. Either we keep following urges or we exercise our brains to hold it back to mould its strength for more productive use. A delicate sixth sense of sensitivity impalpably emerges to guide us through various kinds of systems for processing better futures. The more we discover the interdependencies of applied thinking the greater becomes our confidence to commit our selves to concurrent and consensus based choices about exercising our concerns for all round growth.

It is evident that virtual reality formation is a very carefully composed mind map made up of many systemic wholes. *The research slot* is the continual search for contents that examine and extend notions of wholeness and its parts.

Scientific studies show us that we are made up of different types of cellular particles of matter that are constantly moving to propel our bodily activities. Live atoms are affected by neurons to form synapses of thought very much like the winds that emanate from variations of heat and moisture. Attractions and appeals are picked up by the senses to spark off the instincts that seek satisfaction through energized pressures to act. Genetic codes, geographic features, changing seasons, the food and water we consume, the air we breathe, all affect the way we imagine, feel and perform as private people bound to public scrutiny.

The *action slot* locates essential requisites such as quantities of products and consumers, different types of workers and administrative needs such as infrastructures and facilities, equipment and tools to enable supplying work orders. Designated instructors and skill building exercises need to be undertaken by different categories of workers. Entrepreneurship roles involve complex business sense to make deals, organize sales and distribution and get sanctions from policy makers.

The *presentational slot* in the multi faceted web lists facts, discusses options, notes differences, grades the gathered information to suit a target group of viewers, and uses sequences of real or simulated images to tell the truth. Explanations have to be simple and precise about saying what is important in dialogues that can be easily understood by learners. A conversational friendliness can pass through a maze of thought without straining the receivers. Recalls and reiterations enhance reflective consolidation and lead to confirmations thereby encouraging confident commitment to interactive endeavor.

The constant pursuit of divulging formats of knowledge needs to build trust by keeping the promises that are made. We need to gather enormous stores of ways for being courteous, kind and gentle as we sincerely deal with others. Many friendly alliances have to be proposed and promoted. A lot of courage is needed to develop habits for putting others before ourselves. We discover how thought reinvents itself in rhythmically re-winding or fast forwarding our experiences to suggest better ways of working upon out problematic issues. The adducing of interpretative intervention is like a set of keys to release the restrictive problems that block our ways in expressing our selfhood.

Despite the numerous powers we have to think about many systems for progress we have to turn to The Divine Creator we believe in as the generator of all systems to guide us in redefining and refining our systems of thinking/acting. We always want attention and unconditional love but that is a dream; the reality is made up of bits and pieces that come and go but the desire and the striving is always present.

Our role plays can be urges that are impulsive about tackling conflicts or they can be controlled to attain longer lasting all round growth. We are so involved in the exerting of brain energies that we forget that the essence of living a life lies in the love and concern we have for other sources of energy. The movement from the near to the far is governed by the sap of trust which is rooted in traditions of belief and grows into pathways revealed by the conscience and the memory. Ever widening and inclusively integrative all encompassing circuits form the cycles of growth that lead us to fascinating journeys in self exploration. The quality of the contribution we can make to serve in a scenario of interaction has much greater significance for giving a satisfactory sense of identity formation than any momentary gratification can give. Digital pointers also get power from the way communicators frame philosophies into the scripts they prepare for sharing. Dreams are valid guide posts but circumstances make them happen. Conversations begin within us and we learn to express what we know, feel and enact in different types of formal languages. Many non-formal body languages add power when used in local culturally framed dialects.

The interplay of drives, skills, health, wealth and our temperamental differences is the basic web of holistic awareness for building the creativity that opens possibilities for dealing with the fellowships that sustain life. Discussion groups are essential for guiding us. It is only after getting a chance to observe great dialectic encounters between people that we learn to use our potential for becoming more competent in performing different kinds of action demands. Policy and polity are the most important factors that civilize wild and weak human activists. It is only the well established service rendering infrastructures that facilitate progress. While conventional norms become some kinds of models state institutions prevalent in sets of collective habitats provide the actual opportunities that enable good growth for inhabitants.

The perfect model of fusion comes from noting how different cellular entities mingle in amazing harmony to give us the energies to survive and sustain life, to love and lead to maintain life. Our bodies are made up of living cells that are fortified by flows of breath. Component elements such as brain, bone and muscle systems fuse and get re-generated by absorbing the energy elements in liquid and solid food to enrich the streams of blood that nourishes all other vital organs. The brain needs rich blood to guide the circuits of intelligent thinking to form visions and versions for taking part in sustaining life and living by taking sets of role responsibilities very seriously and faithfully.

Our words seem to arise from a funnel of deep understanding that bores through overlapping layers of specific meanings to stimulate us into making suitable responses for carrying out obligations that gradually lead to the good life.

The *applied* contributing to on-going existence relies upon the principle of equity and harmony in adding to a familiar design that keeps recurring. Themes gather different topics to frame units of interactive progression by triggering the scenes that enact role plays.

- Synergy is a cohesive and concurrent mingling of different kinds of reasons and causes, motives and skills, instructions and wishes, dreams and capabilities to lead us towards rendering service to life.
- Cybernetics is the leadership or followership design that makes us handle the difficulties of processing our humanism. A probe into surface realities and hidden sub texts affect even the factual understanding of environments. Dialogues emphasize certain features and factors about structures, events and efforts. New choices for situation management should incorporate a sense of time by exploring the timeliness of a stimulus and its probable result.
- Contents of communicated offerings have to suit prevailing

fashions for conducting sets of relationships to enable us to form the structures that govern our dealings for the production and distribution of goods.

- Social conventions and civil laws enable people to help themselves and others by voluntarily accepting rules and the regulations pertaining to lawful schemes.

Personal interests always have a public dimension for setting dialogue into patterns of progress. We make adjustments with others as we have to carry them along as equal contributors to the practices that establish progress. Faith in the value being upheld by our chosen expression affects the sincerity that illuminates what we are sharing.

Audio-visual digital creation is a system of multi and cross systems of diverse growth designs to be acquired as a skill of living. Each system intermingles with another and a set of multiple thought movements is composed. Very much like a painted "mandala" more configured patterns open out more worthwhile exchanges. The urge to frame sets of formatted thoughts is the spiritual force that opposes the chaos of differentiations and the unbridled freedom we intelligent thinkers have to strive to control.

Batches of teacher trainees form teams to prepare digital materials. An interconnected web page is a platform for using different kinds of human skills and wills. Given the complexities inherent in defining selfhood and the striving for holistic growth this is a very challenging venture. While sponsors are needed to cover the very high costs of preparing a modular set the public relations approach is needed to establish the systematic creation of modules. A web of joint ventures and memorandums of undertaking for delegating different working duties is put into the product making and sharing circuit. All choices are based on the consensus that is accepted by members. A team of members having different kinds of expertise have to spare a lot of time to execute a good quality teaching tool.

- The team decides upon who are the agencies involved to participate in the entire circuit of preparing materials, funding the expenditure that will be incurred in finalizing the venture and how the product will be used.
- The team plans the detailed nature of the skill-sets required for performing different kinds of tasks and decides which member can take charge of implementing an action agenda according to a format that is pre defined and set into slots and sections of implementation.
- The team allocates tasks in voluntarily accepted democratic ways to manage the digital whole.

Notions of form, style and effectiveness expect us to share general ideas first and then present details to establish the pragmatics of progress. Moods that affect the way we receive logical propositions can be specially built to make difficult structures easier to handle.

Politeness, honesty, truth, affection, beauty of form and a spirit of affection with regard to the compulsions of the other and the reminder about what is valid decorates our communication of thoughts. Patterns of logical and holistic interacting have to cope with constant conflicts, chaotic conditions, suffocating expectations and antagonistic jealousies. Strong beliefs give a lot of self confidence but they can also come across in exaggerated and strident over positive expressions. Habits arising from temperaments can be replenished or changed to make us better players in the games of life.

We work upon the anxiety that triggers the way we choose to develop circuits of co-operative parts and wholes of effort. Forces that help to integrate differences go deep down to the fundamental roots of an issue to locate the harmonizing essence that is the humaneness gifted to us as a soul spirit of conscience.

Teachers have always been trained to have great respect for all by carefully noting the milieu in which learning strategies can be accepted by receivers. The digital medium requires a patient and persistent sense of evident and invisible connection building at all levels of production to give a sensible shape to the deep desires that make us help others.

Chapter Four

Orientation Towards the Digital Mode of Teaching

To "Teach" is a natural urge for intelligent human thinkers who have to play their parts in flowing systems of interactively implemented orders for living. Human actors receive all kinds of information which they keep placing in bunches of regulated segments as ready references to nurture life. Functions have to be continuously performed by paying attention to condition related thinking which is derived by interconnecting some theoretical ideas with familiar and effective practices. Teaching is all about guiding others in seeing how a "subject" is welded together with an "object" through a chosen mode of "interaction" to process some kind of useful and good growth. Professional teaching is a highly systematic probe into some themes for sharing sociologically valid useful knowledge with others to help people in selecting efficient pathways for dealing with life.

The digital mode captures the working awareness of the world as sets of inputs about attaining some kinds of progress to manage the partnership activities within which we live our lives.

Teachers have always been geared towards guiding persons in all round growth and this is now possible through a multi slotted format for integrating diversities into patterns of concurrent education. The digital design is a grand system that brings together co-related sub systems to tease our perceptive intelligence. Different aspects, diverse approaches, fair adjudications, adjustments that have regard for others and a steady faith in the equality of human rights are the foundations for creative interaction. The wonder and the adventure of learning more and seeking new directions for striving to make a mark in the world remains a supreme goal for preparing a holistic digital unit. Visual sequences open domains to affect the personal aims as role playing portions that mingle to frame a slice of life. Effective guidance acquires an impact to the extent to which it adds to familiar experiences in prescriptive ways.

Each audio-visually prepared digitally communicated unit works upon the core premise that life is processed as sets of demands and supplies. A code of situation specific value directs the choices we make to serve the cause we portray by our uttered, written, visually pictured and bodily felt communications. A span of effort is limited by specific knowledge about sets that can be used for designing the shared tasks and the general value coding that leads up to a a desirable goal.

We use all kinds of meanings to build relationships that establish some kind of service by contributing to on-going systems by communicating ideas of growth within a situated encounter. Positions within sets of relationships affect the limits of possibility within which we communicate. Professional teacher training becomes highly sophisticated as it is holistic not only about matters of common concern but also about learning how to use the infinite possibilities that computer technologies provide. Each field of practical discipline has its own principles to lead us to managing finite existence. Values are noted as the bases for establishing the infinite visions that lead to the finite evolutionary progress of persons as partners.

Digital holism looks upon awareness as an innate energy that can be enlarged and extended through versions of thought-as-and-in-routines of actions that accept new designs to maintain the flows of existence. Holistic teaching skills germinate from better vocabularies about "verbal orders". The object is to be noticed as a desirable objective. People need to be seen and shown as working-benefactors as well as the beneficiaries of work done by other humans. There are no limitations as the "subject" is an open goal seeking a range of objectives that become much desirable aims. We draw attention to many interconnected chains of inclusive thinking to satisfy legitimate human ambitions by using a mixture of multimedia skills. Ambitions are embedded into the work skills that enable us to understand and process "verbs" of working schedules. At all times we envisage the multi-purpose ranges of viable paradigms and their ramifictions. Output/input reality considers and contains essential items for growth after collaborating with others.

The digital spectrum moves between perceptions that are attractive, beautiful, organized, utilitarian and productive structures for taking livelihood management into new futures. Digital guidance builds roles by clarifying some routes after duly reflecting upon possibilities for changing some negative conditions, giving instructions for taking up difficult tasks, upholding justice and equity, and very patiently making allowances for people having different abilities.

The digital mode uses a huge variety of languages to interlink flowing movements of interaction in pictorial, textual and verbalized ways. A lot of conflicts, fears, and impulses need to be countered and this can be done by stressing upon an abundance of orderly positive self controlling images. Some preparatory basics are firstly, teachers have to work upon very critically evaluated perspectives about using different approaches to an issue to fulfill many ranges of objectives.

Secondly, graphic scenario developing skills are required to encapsulate intertwined images to manage different types of role-playing responsibilities. Thirdly, a team spirit is to be developed as a lot of artwork has to be done by highly skilled computer specialists. While teachers can evolve their own creativity to undertake some aspects of design it is best to get help when needed. The highly competitive globally connected digital world exerts an overwhelming tension that needs to be managed by finding ways to reduce stress.

Structures to signify positions are imbued with duties for pacing moves to mingle with others and merge their creative talents with the widening horizons of multi tasking to achieve excellent results.

Narrated texts are indicators to suggest meanings that focus upon some realistic pathways to progress. The old blackboard configurations become stories to show how expectations have their own sequels to serve as models. Mood spreading music enhances impact when it echoes the feelings underlying dialogues. Titles and captions are entered to classify the kaleidoscope of images. Felt sources of tension and energy are visually captured as symbolic indices about the truth made visible through body languages. Viewpoints are placed as alternative choices to direct live dealings to manage interactive growth.

Story lines can be traditional, real or simulated notifications that adjust localized traditions with deep universally relevant moral conventions. Conditions that prevent progress and the facilities that establish task taking are easily noted. The difficulty and the challenge of intervention in an ongoing dialogue is rooted in the socially emoted energizing of the enthusiasm to act. It is here that creative appeals must be made to strengthen positive thinking by fusing different audio-visual languages. The energy of passion that can be captured in the digital format has to be so powerful that it can persuade us to change the way we chart a course of action.

Our dialogues to open educative moves are distillations of the ethical principles of transpersonal value which creatively and uniquely color our interactions. These come from personally held strong trusts and beliefs, a religious dimension of faith that accepts categorical imperatives of seeking the truth, being just and law abiding, loving others and making sacrifices and pursuing beauty in creative ventures. Propriety and helpfulness get reflected as courtesies towards different others and as regard for conventions about manners of behavior to suit an occasion. Setting of routines is very important and rituals have to be respected.

Techniques and styles to suit the technological tools being used are the skeletons upon which a teaching module is built. A montage is a detailed choreographing of the composite design that draws attention to the wide arrays of contents. Each sequence is a distinctive, clear, sharp and pointed convincing statement made to appeal to the fusions of thoughts that can spread enthusiasm among receivers to make positive efforts to nurture growth. We remind ourselves of the objectives of our efforts and "teach" ourselves to get fresh perspectives.

- Multimedia modules guide viewers in relatively complete cycles of labor to manage their interventions in flows of systematic civil orders. Themes are chosen to represent some type of progress that is examined and understood, explained and revealed, explored and exposed in many different ways to construct a pattern of living life. A unit projects some purpose to produce a consumable product in terms of all its component elements such as substances, matter, materials and methods set in steps and stages of work. The scope of the unit carries its own weight to determine the quantitative dimensions of the quality building outreach.

- The sensibility to comprehend parts and wholes of some kinds of orders to interlink them is the heart centre of digitally mind mapped array of mind mapped understanding. Data about different work sections is gathered, scanned and set into tasks to show how growth can be independently organized for action. Structures are built by breaking a set of knowledge into sequential construct that can inspire an abiding love and concern for fellow beings.
- Slots are set as scripts to hold attention in exposing designs of thought to establish richly meaningful impact. At the focal centre is a deep concern for helping people to manage their lives with dignity, vigor, valor and versatility. We compile different topics as short story lines in an inclusive scenario of reality formation. Vivid visual graphics enhance the features and factors of logical systems to infer interactive growth. Shapes and size matter; so each section has its own style, tempo, weight, and inferential features that merge to maintain the harmonized qualitative dimensions within the overall scope of the shared venture.

A lot of team work is needed at every level to process the

forming of units. The first stage is to locate skilled workers who can satisfy skill sets that are identified. Methods and modalities for performing role plays are core skills that are noted for enlisting members into teams. Working conditions, administrative set ups, quality controls, financial and infrastructural provisions and just and fair trade practices are climates for getting work "done" within the electronic medium. The team has to be very much mature because openness is a fundamental principle of audio-visual communication. It is necessary to capture the market for getting inputs in open-ended tasks from the "outside".

An effective team is formed by people who have the right talents and the right attitudes for being efficient in specific skills by being large hearted enough to welcome outside interventions. Training incumbents in acquiring the temperaments that are needed for the job is a very subtle exercise that needs psycho-metric evaluation and casual encounter management.

Audio-visual teaching encircles variety and reiterates commitment to reach out to receivers who are conditioned to follow their own habits of thinking. The gestural and emotionally expressed cultural conventions for expressing belief in traditional patterns are images depicting the changing bio-rhythms that affect the way we accept ritual messages and color them with our popular contemporary fashions. Primieval tribal art forms provide valuable lessons in bio-rhythmic longings and their satisfactions to the confusion ridden fashions of contemporary co-existence. Many levels and stages in circuits of effort energies need different experiential expressions of effort for playing roles.

Exercises To Develop Digital Competence

Content creation needs team work because only some aspiring teachers have attained a lot of expertise in developing a specific type of required skill to complete an obligation to a consumer.

We always make scrap books of sketches, observations and the things that reveal the artistic competence that frame in a portfolio.

Those having an abiding interest in music and lyrics have the competence to make great sound bytes for displaying moods.

Those having an interest in pictures and sensitive feelings can find their future in taking still photos and become cinematographers.

If you are gifted with a love of linguistics to make life dramatic you can be a good script writer.

If you react strongly to civil rights and governmental policies you can be a reporter or a journalist to educate others by making messages about events as news.

A fascination for adventure and travel makes you a good anchor for geography-cum-culture illustrative anthropological travels.

Skill combinations need operative continuity on a dedicated level to attain strengths to format graphically designed self expression to work on professional platforms for delivering creative products.

Holistic viewpoints about genuine notions of deep rooted fellowship feeling come easily when we rely upon a disciplining of the self by adhering to the wisdom taken from the religion we ascribe to. Prayer helps us to be steadily and patiently supportive of the characteristic idiosyncrasies of each other. A non-judgmental critique can uncover the fearless freedom of the artist who must get into the habit of upholding creative team spirit.

We need to understand world making by observing the following basic features that affect learning for living life:

- The facilities provided by political, legal and social regulations to extend personal progress,

- The factions that exist and the fallacies that accompany our fancies and our fears,
- The differences of opinions about undertaking responsibilities and how to be very sure of your facts to convince others,
- The perfecting of communicative strategies to become fluent and feelingly manage the personality differences that will exist,
- The control over short term pleasures to make some sacrifice for larger, more important gains,
- The good humored taking of criticism and the gentleness in offering it as well as giving reasons for your personal opinion.

How Digital Information Brings Greater Fellowship

Digital dialogues are business centered in a world of opportunity and chance as the mind flits and files some features that can be fused into flows of growth. The portal is the powerhouse for revealing potential energy for open utilization. A digital posting has to be designed to fit into a spectrum that specifies the coverage of facts. Job seeking can be more precise when there are agencies to facilitate the searches.

The validation for excelling in a skill set to nurse an aspiration needs proof which can be directly posted. Validation is possible through portals such as Facebook and Youtube.

The World Wide Web, www establishes connectivity by using hyper text markup languages to develop universal resource locations known as html, and url, Blogs and collaborative networks have expanded domains for reaching out to everyone who learns to use the resources with total self understanding about claims that are authentic, sincere and available for unusual usages.

In conclusion the practices for advancing holistic multi-media teaching are as follows:

- The deal and its elements are to be carefully clarified as types of exchanges.
- Operations are spelt out in terms of the form, shape and size of the set of benefits.
- Instruments and instructions about modalities of working in methodical steps and stages is the content spread of a proposed project.
- The system for gathering inputs from partners and the expected outcomes of each type of partnership has to be clearly outlined.
- Script setting explores duties as clearly stated expectations and circumscribes the factual use of the features that are being noted. The recurring production of methods to be consistent about co-operative growth reframes incidents as instances that suggest instructive reinforcements as guided situations. Like an aside in a drama covert values to suit complicated choices can be highlighted through some special design features. Each subject based element has to be true to the principles that hold the specific use that is being projected in a digital unit.
- Pre-project requirements for getting suitably trained human-power, infrastructural facilities, and precise task analyses are outlined to get support and funds for large ventures.
- On going participation in delivering undertakings demands a very positive creative leadership commitment to fulfill the objectives being undertaken through the proposed project.
- Maintaining records, sharing new information, highlighting

successes, giving support to incumbents and answering queries from the receivers of project details is a basic practice for ensuring the futuristic design of the networks that a digital unit ensures for freely opted participative progress.

What to do about the digital teachers' own doubts, fears, worries and uncertainties? Some guidelines are being stated:

- *Use the head but follow the intuition,* be critical but don't let it show till you have found a new direction and an empathetic way to be more effective.
- *Anger control builds the role,* you have to always enlighten and inspire, enthrall and elevate.
- *Stop and cool off,* you have to do something else, look again, seek some more information.
- *Learn to love with your heart,* open a dialogue in a happy form and the smiles will help others and you too.
- *Be open and hide the pain* you may feel, talk about tough issues and problems with friends.
- *Be faithful to your innermost value syndromes,* keep researching to preserve the microscopic version of a macrocosmic vision.

Chapter Five

Meditating to Make Webs of Holistic Thinking

Humans are programmed to imitate what they appreciate. Since there are multitudes of options how do we find our way to make good choices? There is a philosophical approach to life that not only evaluates events but goes deeper to reinterpret intuitions into working decisions. This leads to an acceptance or a negation of what is known and experienced. We are blessed with multiple ways of processing and revealing our thoughts. Patterns of thought adjust conventions with perceptions to accept some logical structures of action/reaction. The exercising of our intelligence is a very private and scarcely felt shade of will power that examines motives before arriving at conclusions along with the kinds of objectives that are being upheld. Persons have to keep adjusting to the intentions that all players have in a situated set of role playing.

We have to trust a scheme of logical examination when we strive to find satisfactory ways of coping with the divisions and dichotomies of living. Certainty about what option we take to communicate with each other comes from an inner sensing of being truthful, caring, just and correct in beautifully conducting our relationships.

We cannot concentrate on thinking beyond a span of differentials and must let attention wander and return. Fate and fortune is a mystery but feelings and creative work are real events. Life is a series of problems but the determination to deal with them is the tough path that has to be found and taken by relying upon ethical moralities.

The wise thinkers of ancient India have told us how to meditate and act to please others and learn to use the enormous gifts we have to grow in wonderful ways. Choice making is developed from infancy when the child cries or laughs. *Dhrishti* sees surroundings, *Rasa* starts with taste, *Rupa* is distinguished as form, touch is felt as *Sparsa,* scents and smells are noted as *Gandha.* These basic senses are primary spheres for recreating impacts upon each other.

Human life is largely self-controlled as the body emerges in accordance with some bio-genetic principles. Pre-coded mixes of chromosomes gathered from male and female parents give us life.

Great thinkers have said that physical admixtures of the five elements, air, water, light, wind and the earth, operate through the five senses to create, affect and condition life. Science has corroborated this core foundation of existence by studying cell structures as substances that move as ejected particles that regenerate as new compounds of charged energies to open new types of inter-intra activities. Visually we can see that rays are emitted and synapses transmit colluding chemical compounds in recurring waves for live mutative dynamics. Nature is programmed evolution that sustains itself through the transformative processes that are always working. However there are limited capacities for procreation, preservation, decay, destruction and rebirth. This is a cosmic cycle that affects life as living.

The wise sages have told us that when "*sneha*", love is

glimpsed, "*viveka*", discrimination as idea, develops "*vicharadhara*", stream of thought, that becomes "*karma*", action. "*Nishtha*", force of energy executes action and "*Shradha*", faith, spreads benefits and losses. *Dhyana* is a set of *dhagas* and *dharas* to build *kritis* according to *Dayitvas*, of responsibilities. Intellectual understanding and emotional power ignites bodily labor in physical terms and in subtle, hidden, innate intuitions of the spirit of energy deep within the body. *Meditation is a study in living up to a faith* to give us the confidence to strongly make our inner journeys explicit. The trust that is meditated is a subtle directive that highlights a concern before we seek and find its significance as meanings to release messages. Intelligence mediates premeditated thoughts by remaining within some boundaries to bind them in order to bond with different receivers. Priorities exist and routines are ways of giving due importance to some basic requirements of survival and growth. Complex problems goad us to find solutions.

There are numerous ways of meditating about contradictory and complex realities and among them "*Panchadisha-darshan*" is a classical ancient tradition for experiencing the intricacies of life and living. The philosophy known as *Vedanta, which literally means the end of knowledge* is a process that directs understanding in five slots has been very succinctly revealed by the great guru, *Sri Shankarcharya*. All existence can be understood by placing thoughts into five dimensions to format existence as operational practice.

Life is made up of five elements. Matter is the "earth" slot that makes our bones and muscles. The light and heat of the sun and the sky is the source of the energies that move in different channels in various ways. Wind and water push and change the energies that move in the body. The air we breathe is the vital resource behind all sources of action energy. Food, clothes, homes, commodities are derived from the feelings of love and concern that self communing thinkers interconnect. The blending of pre meditated faith to produce material objects manages mutual co-existence. Since there is a multitude of options how do we find our way?

Faith is an Inextricable Element of Intelligence

Faith has to be established to design our own forms for contributing to ways of living. A norm is a mysterious system to develop the faith that can give us more satisfactory control over the tensions and pressures of collaborative life living? While the details are specific there is a generalized overview that sets the mood for accepting a methodology. Instructions for using instruments need to make place for the individualistic nature of creativity in following procedure.

A direct dealing is conditioned by a very broad-based system of clues through which we can locate the most effective and good ways of managing the situations we face. There is a philosophical approach to life that goes beyond the action specific evaluations we make as well as includes them.

Faith is an invisible hotline that energizes us to form satisfactory identities as we rove and realize the undercurrents of universal values that civilize our relationships with others.

Faith is the spirit of the soul that makes us meditate and guides us as we must act and react to deal with different kinds of encounters.

Faith is an infinite indefinable spirit that controls the finite ways in which we get bound together in harmonious ways to manage our interdependent existence.

Faith is dynamic and creative as it can cut across layers of preconceived thinking when we find a wonderful new way of looking at matters.

Faith is a fountain that quells our thirst for adventure despite the trials and tribulations we face.

Faith triggers progress in the world by expanding our controls over our lives as we learn to become better partners.

Faith thrives on order, balance, harmony, and a sense of beauty and love.

Faith gives us a sense of togetherness and belonging that can be so strong that we are willing to make sacrifices to keep holding on to what has been revealed to us.

Dialogue is bound by domains of faith that develop contents for selecting what to communicate with different others to serve a purpose. Designs of expression are descriptive in direct ways. Information inter-connects some divisions to functions through different kinds of efforts so as to sustain spans of living. Possibilities emerge from past experiences and futuristic probabilities. Knowledge is built upon certain formulae:

- Intellectual trust can be horizontally extended by adding facts to explain an area of information,
- Emotional intensity gives the energy of enthusiasm to execute a task or get pained by a failure,
- Vertical dimensions of probes into layers of thought cut across different types of understanding to locate a sense of completeness and totality,
- Lateral thinking exposes different possibilities for attaining objectives,
- Mechanical thinking establishes step by step methods of cumulative labor for making a product,
- Circular thinking moves between some radial divisions that look at an issue in different ways to compose thoughts,
- Mathematical thinking constructs scientific essences of ratio and proportion to configure numbers for correctly implementing tasks,

- Cyclic thinking cuts across patterns of knowledge and expands viewpoints,
- Cultural thinking provides models to indicate the shape of struggling to establish a collective consciousness about dealing with destiny.

In classical Indian understanding of thought the conglomerate of mind and energy has been described as Bodh-bal. The mental force works as gunabheda, which is the qualities we are given as differences to develop our identity. Stithis are states of existence, Sthayibhava is steady thinking, Kaal is a span of time and Sthana denotes the placed position to perform Anukool Sewa. Kala is the way service is rendered according to the artifice that construes and constructs the art of playing a role. At the centre is Aakarshan (attraction) having a distinct irradiating particle as an entity of creative karyakriti, task-taking. Swadhyaya is self devised control over ones skills for exploring ways of contributing after understanding varieties, variables and vagaries in executing ventures.

The *Panchadhrishti* provided by the senses becomes a base for deciphering the *Panchakaranas* that combine with *Panchagunas* as he *Aadhaar*, (foundations) of the *Aakaars*, (forms) in which the life force performs *Aavishkaars*, (discoveries) as per its *Aakaankshas*, (desires) *its Ashwasans,* (certitudes) *and its Adhikaars*, (rights) *as the Jeevdhari vyakti, (living being),* within the cosmic *Vyapti. (Space). Naras and Madas,* are males and female entities who fuse extracts from their reproductive organs and new creation takes place. Fusion thus seems to be the key to life.

For the purpose of digital teaching we need to undertake some basic ranges philosophies to meditate upon our favorite ways of stimulating others and responding to their expressions.

With whom are we bonding? What are we supposed to do?

How are we connecting the facts we are explaining as the means to performing some functions that are expected from us?

Are we looking at facts as situation managing formations and blending them into the life style patterns familiar to our target receivers?

Are we aware of the expectations that push us in overcoming our ignorance, weaknesses and mood variations?

Are we finding very attractive and direct ways to make the growth design last longer?

Are we suggesting alternatives for selecting our unique styles to fit into the changes that we want for making people help themselves and each other?

Are we accosting common fears and taking up on the fancies that people have? Are we confronting wrong methods, misuse of power and hurting sensibilities?

Do we remain honest and truthful, cheerful and polite, kind and popular while addressing receiver groups?

All matters end in the inevitability of the cycle that regenerates vital interaction by making us think objectively about all that is dear to us. At the same time the things that we need, seek, love and try to arrange for attaining safe and secure progress for life acquire enormous importance.

For us humans many rigid habits get formed as we frame our beliefs into seeking various kinds of benefits. We can be bold and benign as we cloak our desires by wearing the garb of power to make our meanings attractive or we can do nothing and become lazy and dull. The core component of faith that we exert is an immaculate concept for unlimited growth that can change the most deeply entrenched habits. We are blessed with the gift of sacrificing our own interests to sustain the good life for others by exercising some of the vast ranges of productive interactions that we have been blessed with.

Good health strengthens all the energies. When emotions are strong the heart beats change their tempo. Enthusiasm entertains desires but exaggerated passions depress. Frequency of demands and their control is like day and night. Both states have to be welcomed. A micro-processing inference opens one state and closes the other but both define and determine procedures about progress. An emotional cleansing gives way for a new cycle in the materialistic constructing of the world.

Exercises in breathing control undue tensions. Rhythmic ways of exhaling and inhaling have an impact across the mind-body feeling spectrum. Vigor affects frequencies and locates harmony to seek progress in peaceful ways. A divine trajectory of consciousness is the grand design that is echoed in our communicative activities. Numerous free radical evolutions are framed in sets of interdependent boundaries to control types of positioned cells as forces and flows of order.

Kaliedoscopes for Meditating

Meditation automatically arises as we make visual collages, give them oral or written meanings of value and worth and bind them into our love of life.

Kathas, (Stories), Paintings, Crafts, Performances, Religion (as prayer, purifying rite, sanctuary, japa, dhyana, guna gyana,)

Simply Adages are Mini Meditations

Thoughts go wild, tame them; Feelings go wild, change them; Actions go wild, mend them; Partners go wild, talk to them; Wishes go wild, stop them; Problems become issues, resolve them; Keep moving, happy or sad, it does not really matter, plod on and you matter.

Highly sophisticated compositions for using academically valid knowledge can be derived by locating and combining sets of spheres for directing attention. A grand circuit called a *"mandala"* has been artistically devised in different cultural traditions as a disciplined way of meditating about parts and wholes of existence. It is meditation alone that joins together the bits and pieces of perceiving the world as world making.

The Kannada poet Basavanna, who lived in the twelfth century AD wrote this wonderful poem:

The rich may build temples to the Lord,
But what can I, a poor man do?
My body is the mansion, my legs are the pillars,
My head is a shining cupola of gold,
Oh lord of the melting rivers, the standing ever shall fall,
The moving ever shall stay.

Kathas
Paintings
Images
Documentaries

- Performed Arts
- Fine Arts
- Crafts Arts
- Film
- Religion
  as prayer
  as ritual
  as dhyana
  as guna gyana
  as purification
  as fasting to control passion
  as sanctuary

Temple

Figure 5.1 Kaleidoscope for Meditating

Chapter Six

Designing Inclusive Multi-Media Learning Modules

Humans have a burning desire to make others accept the operative patterns that are successful for working out the interdependence of existence. In the previous chapters we have explained how real existence is a continuous building of scenes to reveal our concerns about all kinds of problems and tackle them with great acumen and courage. Multi-media modules tackle complex issues after undertaking a lot of research and gathering data which has to undergo careful analysis to open new directions for finding better remedies to harness rapidly changing work scenarios. While cognition takes us into new realms of concept formation we promote only those notions that are acceptable to others. Verbal skills are linked to emotional energies which drive people by "cultivating" interpersonal skills. Technical expertise is essential for using computers in skillful ways to improve job opportunities in an open-ended globally innovative scenario. The search for sound and longer lasting paths to build new kinds of careers is a challenge that probes deeply into building contacts to get contracts in an open market. Arts as artistry in effectively communicating new ideas for growth work through the sharp acumen that builds new kinds of working partnerships. Rigid discipline is essential for building competence in a lot of multi-disciplinary exercises to give satisfactory results in new ventures. Venture capital is a new type of patronage that supports innovations and builds connections between different types of players so that new star-ups can be efficiently set-up.

Dialogues are transitory states of controls over events and eventualities that encode the movements that take place all around us. Assumptions about social and personal progress emerge from in depth thinking about different sets of presumptions about the parts to be gathered to form wholes to give a new birth to something or to replace what has decayed or has lost its usefulness. Although there are many explicit areas of effort to be organized in great detail many hidden depths need to be uncovered through reiterated patterns of understanding what has to be done and how to choose tiny ways of doing big things. While impulses are essential for making dynamic moves they need support from qualitative strengths, which come through habits of working hard to patiently locate strategies out of wide-ranging and deep rooted logical thinking.

A multi media module is an *epistemology* in itself as it spans diverse ranges of information to manage operations on the ground in attractive and appealing ways. While facts are listed a complete analysis demands a deep study of the factors that affect a problem area. Findings pave the ground for trans-mutating available resources to open up specific services for micro managing precious human resources. Talent hunting takes the central space when there are masses of job seekers and employers. Learning becomes a tough self discipline, so the ways in which we must learn becomes more a matter of guidance and counseling for helping the self learning individual. Multi media languages are both policies and practices which further fashion themselves as communicative patterns. A very rapid grasp of multi-linguistic designs becomes the foundation for opting to pursue interest based ways of expressing oneself. The differently competent team becomes the centre point for divulging multidisciplinary knowledge as a whole to be used in parts as required by the player joining a partnership.

New patterns for contemporary growth consciousness are very complicated exercises in making enthusiastic movements to do what is expected from us and what we have dedicated ourselves for attainment. It is the *Spirit* deep within us, somewhere, that clarifies concepts about living our lives with ease by holding together the notions that we ourselves gather to solve our problems. A lot of worry and the resultant tension can make us desperate but there are some very sudden bursts of fresh enthusiasm that bring us back to our duties with fresh vigor. Meditation precedes mediation as it is some intuition that gives humans the green signal to carry on proceeding with our goals and perform our duties to others in considerate ways.

The need to please and persuade persons to initiate new self expression to work in unison with others is the dominant feature for framing oral and pictorial "languages" about doing better things in better ways. Each block of work is entered into a flow that opens a venture from its concept to its fruition. There are new systems to be opened and there are many that are to be obeyed while preparing an inclusive projection of desirable progress. Different policies are to be framed and permissions are to be sought from policy making caretakers. Sets of personnel are drafted to creatively organize and implement the product developing details. Publicity and public relations for marketing ideas and getting support for action plans is an essential part of the deals that have to be established. The budgeting of large ventures is a specialized task needing expert guidance for getting sponsors and stake holders. Very often it is the pursuit of efficiency by itself that incites the mind to be sharper, makes behavior more pleasant, establish strong values of justice and fair play, be loyal towards bosses, remain truthful and dedicate oneself to the cause being upheld by the work that is undertaken.

Developing Inclusive Digital Units about Life Management

Human minds traverse pegs of duties and follow inner feelings to build definitive webs of inputs to attain desirable outputs. Images are patterns that lay down well planned parameters for implementing tasks as specific propositions for undertaking strategic interaction. Collectives of inhabitants in the global open participative world order need very definitive ways of working upon sets of services. The business managerial approach dominates the mass produced knowledge for making provisions available to all. Mind maps copy the spider who weaves webs to wander in and remain safe. Brainstorming is done to identify radiating branches about some significant matter or issue by making notes about constitutive components that laterally reveal basic facts and associated features. Sub-sections of consideration for more detailed analyses are invoked within the sequences of interactive situations. Dialogues both follow conventions and give them new dimensions. The rough graphic is like a drawing board for collecting together the notions that have become apparent and bonding them into presentable projections for addressing others. Certain boundaries are laid to secure the paths that are to be traversed to get a full picture of the processes to be followed as sets of procedures by different players.

Studies to promote holistic awareness in digital modes of information sharing are based on some foundations for building patterns of mutual growth. These are as follows:

- Working relationships are decisively implemented in five dimensions; *mental, physical, emotional, condition-based and interest-centered parameters.*
- *Situated encounters* are presented as *strings of episodes* to portray scenes to help people in understanding scenarios within which mutual co-existence can be undertaken. Relationship expectations are divulged in formal and non formal ways to satisfy various kinds of basic demands and common desires.
- Various types of accomplishments and responsibilities are required to facilitate frameworks of declarations that have to circumnavigate between different types of culture centered scenarios to deal with the constant search for managing ventures in comprehensive and cohesive ways.
- *Sensitivity training* is a core element in the humane approach towards meeting functional objectives. Aims need to be formed as sparks to brighten the flames that make a mark upon the receivers of messages.
- *Skills and competence* in using conventions of form and styles to create expressions according to cultural heritages and traditional forms give greater strength and scope to the self directing impact that a digital unit can provide.

Designs for Learning How to Create Digital Units

We begin with formal Language acquisition and combine it with non-formal social milieus in which we place ourselves. The alphabet stage itself is the stepping stone for building notions to frame concepts in real contexts of expressing ourselves. Symbols are signs to make words that make linguistic "sense" when used in combinations of utterances. Vowels join consonants to make words that are developed as sentences to express meanings. Relationships emerge as connections between nouns are connected with verbs to make statements. Demands and supplies, statements and reports, questions and replies, explanations and exclamations are linguistic formats for affirming social regulations, adopting them and adapting life styles to adjust with them. Digital mixes of oral, written and pictorial languages open notions as efforts enacted in time and place while working out different obligations towards socio-politically established sets of partnerships.

The sensing of a present reality works through a feel for the future that introspects upon the past to give emphasis to a purpose. A hostile atmosphere surrounds the competitive reality of participative existence which can be addressed only by truth and trust to make us determined about the causes we are espousing. Many appeals to the conscience help in making people more conscientious about consciously working for a worthy cause. A page maker in a computer disc holds together a lot of complex information about facts in patterns of sequential images to suggest concurrent approaches for designing life.

The more multipurpose and multi sensory a composition is the greater is the impact it makes. Texts illuminate facts as factors about inputs to get better outputs. Graphs and flowcharts need story lines to enrich different portions of the parameters of the larger main frame. Arguments incorporate numbers of beneficiaries to give economic value to services that support mainstream policies for funding the facilities that lead to progress. A lot of mood building additives of sound, color, music and poetic rhythm provide memory aids. Stories decorate the languages for understanding complex issues and vivid configurations reduce the difficulties in understanding compounded forays of concentrating upon vitally essential factors. A kiosk like digital unit strings together different threads to form live pictures that have the power to evoke better ways of participating in the types of ventures that are the themes being tackled.

Certain movements of actors during encounters need to be highlighted therefore contrasting colors variations in the darkness and brightness, indicative captions and pointers use voice tones and sound effects to enhance the impact of audio-visual teaching. Contents and contexts jointly open negative and positive options as arrays of dealings need to please all kinds of consumers. A subtle undercurrent of decisive choice making is always indicated or gets noted through the body languages of the participants. Since a feel for commitment dominates dialogue, convictions are sensitively presented. Specially decorated and stylized images need to be attractive and sentimental to leave lasting impressions.

Mental exercises to prepare a multi-media exposition need an emotional touch and a sense of moral roots to access spiritual creativity. Empathy building is important as it overlooks small differences that people have which are not as important as the sincerity, or insincerity of body languages. Tensions and contentment are visible through the way gestures are used. The expressions of the face are mirrors of the feelings within us. Culturally established factors like types and styles of dressing, speech patterns and the choice of idioms are outer indicators of the undercurrents of intention that display identities. Character building is largely managed by tactful dialogue used to frame conventions commonly followed in role playing. The use of a region based dialogue gives authenticity to the speech that is chosen by activist human actors.

Layers of impressions re-occur but with changing meanings to suit the usages that situated encounters seek. Many value additions enrich the enthusiasm that makes humans creatively concerned about each other. An invisible rhythm of concentrated attention to frequently desired and required activities can be compared to the recurring seasons that Nature has provided. An overarching aesthetic of sincere fellowship fuses spoken and felt images. Just as objects have shape, size, weight, texture and usefulness abilities acquire potential energies in terms of classical approaches or folk art to be popular and acceptable in an academic commitment to excellence. If a concept benefits others it takes on a mystique that incites the psyche to seek logical solutions for implementing visions as versions of interaction. The drudgery of routines is highly vulnerable to careless speech acts so silent contemplation is most important for devising a large plan of arduous responsibilities to produce products.

Digital holism teaches by giving added value of economic gain to invigorate deep thinking and makes us more capable of exposing our innate thoughts in more vivid and pertinent ways. Perceptions about making products by tapping human propensities are very important for all kinds of framers of policies. Notions about creative participation in any venture minutely examine the parts, portions and totalities of usage. At all times form enhances the sensible yarns of trust-in-action that the spider-mind spins. A format that empowers people by sharing a dividend among many other partners opens a sense of having a stake which makes difficult endeavor worthwhile. Universal values have to be frequently noted to evoke cultures of convictions which result in making sacrifices to pursue self driven dreams.

Basic Design Frameworks for Digital Mediation

Digital holism animatedly confronts processes as live demonstrations of procedures for product creation. An introductory glimpse of a large vision is framed as a set of components. Different divisions for undertaking large work orders are stated as categories and numbered. Sub sections are formed and explained. Images and texts to suit sections are framed as instructions and guidelines. Searches and findings are listed separately and incorporated into the slots of experiential learning that is formatted into slots for interaction by various employees/employers. Provisions are made for situating work areas and giving the equipment and the tools for taking tasks by teams of workers. A lot of detailed practice is needed to produce expected results. Multisensory appeals are used to attract the attention of target audiences. Actual episodes, graphic configurations real life incidents, samples and models are presented, to explain work areas for collaborative team worked professional action. Different kinds of software are available as techniques to design different features for use in a Digital Learning Unit.

The project mode uses graphic aids to explain large ranges of contents as contexts for making contacts with potential participants. The internet is the best way of reaching out to access resources of different kinds. There is much pre-project data to be collected. Surveys reveal the quantum of work that has to be undertaken to serve a collective of users. Photographed evidence, diagrams and flowcharts, location based films, symbolically added on animation, arts and aesthetics of communicating are some ways of making presentations to initiate support for large proposals. Story lines are developed to impart sensitivity training. Pictures are created and texts are added to make sure that very considerate humane behavior accompanies the objectives that are being formed. Sound and light effects, colors, shapes and sizes, patterns and perspectives, props and artistic conventions and cultural features enrich and enhance meanings.

Interfaces between people and their surroundings have to be inferred according to existing conditions to explain set-ups as start-ups, phased structures, sections and sequences for taking on tasks, giving training to employees, arranging supervisory systems to maintain standards of excellence, opening up/down channels for information sharing and up dating strategies to ensure successful operations. Many additives and embellishments make it easier to accept sets of duties as types of loyalties. The spirit of togetherness lies in fusing work items as demands and details, skill-strengths, humane sensitivities and simplified practices to create the mood for voluntarily taking part in following open ended rules about fixing instructions about obligatory responsibilities.

Each unit has a slot to assess needs to configure structures as components, divisions and modalities to attain some objectives at each section of joint working. A story line is developed to show how causes become purposes that are to be sought as segments, stages and phases of inclusive progress. Scenarios skillfully craft networks of order by selectively framing scenes as episodes that project sequences along with consequences to illustrate the dialectics of joint progress. Episodes are compilations of meanings as visuals and directives about systems and systematic to manage a slice of interactive thinking.

Pictures highlight sensations and messages need to be hyped

and reiterated to give importance to the meanings being presented. Artwork is an aesthetic presentation of inherent complexities as contrasts to visually compose foreground acts set in backdrops of real existence. Camera work is built on light effects, shapes and perspectives, color contrasts and staged décor. Oral speech has to match the framed movements in time and the use of other effects. Vocabularies are brief and catchy as the pictures do most of the "talking". Texts narrate as well as highlight imagined versions of perceiving conversational matters. Characters can be real but their state of mind needs superimposed comments and motifs to expose the struggle to attain an envisaged ideal. Sound tracks are added on to highlight the moods that affect the dialectics behind the dialogues.

Messages are presented as background scenarios and foregrounds of focus for letting will-power take its course. Patterns and styles of speech, décor, color and feeling for revealing a thought are delicate fine arts that can ordain a vibrant life to the logical reasoning of the dialogue. Vocabulary is catchy and brief as photographs and short movies do most of the talking. Scripts superimpose reasons in different contexts and notes can be entered. Sketches blend postures to retain a sense of movement to the indices that project growth. Statements expand horizons by blending graphic charts with texts and clips of drawings and photographs, and films are used to give a dynamic vibrancy to topics.

Setting the Multi-Purpose Unit in Specific Slots

Slot 1, Equipment, materials, technological tools and techniques to labor for a purpose are the primary slot areas for undertaking responsibilities to make and deliver goods.

Slot 2, Facts about conditions and training persons to be

effective and efficient at the jobs they undertake is necessary for managing work orders.

Slot 3, Team building by animating skills and exploring aptitudes is the human resource to be developed when exploring digital awareness. Expectations are to be noted as duties and allowances are made for letting conditions affect the ways in which detailed activities are carried out.

Slot 4, Working on models of Deals to manage dealings as instructions and open subtexts that are personal, skill based and emerge from freely chosen value bases. There are no boundaries except the essence and the essentials of bonding to form and frame dialogue.

Slot 5, Many animated semiotics reveal a field of growth as concurrent sets of roles to be taken to gradually attain progress.

How to Develop a Digital Learning Unit

Servers need a lot of guidance based on clear cut norms and standards of work to make role taking for joining flowing orders of civilization workable. *Problems* are both the subjects that incite us to open new futures and the objects that result from inadequacies, dislikes and other mood variations. *Designs* are sets of inferences relying upon diverse references about resources to be sought, provisions to be gathered, and enabling strategies are listed as multi-purpose issues to be resolved, reduced or re-designed. *Contents* are set into assorted boxes that can form action circuits as organized cycles of joint labor. *Operations* are to be carefully defined as phases and stages of task taking. Potential *partners and employees* need very specific details about the work areas that they have to manage or work out.

A venture is thus a series of cohesions which need to be proposed as turn key projects to establish production lines from start to finish. The first screening of quests states the problem and how to address it. From infrastructure management to placements and time bound operations almost half the work is noted. Promotional stances are very important so gains and costs are included as sets of duties and rights to sustain chains of demands and supplies. A check list has to note the following slots to make plans:

- Financial support systems are the preliminary foundations for undertaking large networks of projected activities.
- The gathering and storing of materials and manpower, tools for methods of use and techniques for developing modes of using specific skills to structure sets of regulated tasks is a primary exercise.
- The second screening mixes types of responsibilities by merging work areas with standards of accomplishment for working. Preferences matter a lot while opening positions of work to manage the prosperity being sought. Progress can be impersonally visualized but direct participation has to honor the uniqueness of the persona while producing things for the common good.
- The third slot focuses on building teams of work forces by testing aptitudes to determine abilities while screening operators at entry levels. Specilization and in-house training ensure the managing of details for efficient and time bound deliveries of goods.
- The fourth slot of facilitation and supervision needs to be offer rewards and punishments to use the competitive spirit to maintain standards of efficiency by resolving conflicts between workers. A reiteration of harmonious and peaceful togetherness is a vital inner motivation for arousing the

deep thinking that has to be carefully explicated. Vested interests can be noted only by the conscientious workers who provide the feedbacks can help in reducing losses. Complaint boxes are a great help but only trusted managers should sort them out for taking action.

- The play way game model is very useful in speeding thought processes to give a transpersonal appeal to change dogmatic viewpoints that arise from familiar patterns of doing things. Very often experts get so involved in their special knowledge that they lose sight of the humane needs of working partners and receivers.

Holistic Literacy

We can grasp the significance of thinking before acting if vocabulary building is focused on verbs as learning schedules. Each sentence enacts a decision based on discovering what an action can attain. While a subject serves an object it is the conviction to do something that matters. Holistic thinking uses skills in sharing to achieve desires or satisfy demands. A hint is enough to make eager persons try out their communicative role playing. It becomes much easier to compose dialogues when we experiment with ways of messaging.

- Tend, fend, bend, mend, blend >and send.
- Change, chart, choose, challenge, >and take a chance.
- Road, goad, load, abode, mode, > make an advance.
- Examine, explore, explain, exchange, expose, >to expand, extend.)
- Refer, infer, confer, defer, > prefer.
- Identify, simplify, verify, signify, specify, >to satisfy.
- Interpret, initiate, intervene, inject, >to invent.

- Assist, insist, resist, persist, desist, >to contribute.
- Attract, abstract, impact, tact. >interact.
- Asses, access, advise, appoint, >to contain.
- Address, express, suppress, impress, >activate.
- Define, combine, refine, confine, > assign.
- Initiate, indicate, replicate, invigorate, implicate, > advocate.
- Impose, propose, oppose, depose, >suppose.
- Regulate, relate, emulate, remonstrate, > reciprocate.
- Emulate, speculate, assimilate, stipulate, simulate, > educate.
- Transfigure, transform, translate, transact, transfer, > transcend.
- Consider, confide, contrive, connive,>convert.
- Compare, repair, prepare, impair >consider.
- Contain, consider, compose, convey, complain>confirm.
- Contact, consult, confront, counteract, condemn, > collaborate.
- Connect, confer, correct, contact, contemplate, > control.
- Confirm, conform, convert, concede, constitute, > contract.

Some Fields of New Studies for Digital Skill Building

- Bi-lingual learning for target receivers in non-formal ways.
- Logistics for large work structures to service masses of beneficiaries.
- Life sciences for habitats to be enacted as demands and supplies through convenient trade centers.
- Citizenship concepts set in non-formal models.
- Public private partnerships to render essential services in different sectors.
- Wealth management and its recycling.

- Land usages and holdings for business purposes and housing populations.
- Heritages of culture and tourism.
- Trade and business dealings.
- Vocations and openings for giving and getting services.
- Community welfare management.
- Arts and the support agencies that nurture them.
- Multi-modal Transport facilities.
- Family courts for counseling and guidance.
- Locality management in urban and rural areas.
- Information sharing networks and problem solving on demand.

The Outreach and its Coverage

- The proposal is the first notice and should separately cover all the domains.

The micro level functions are sorted into divisions having specific spheres of task taking.

- Owners and sets of collaborations, > Partnerships and Deals,
- Enablers and Facilitators, >Managers and Duties,
- Trade and Distribution of Products,>Distributors and Dealers
- Memorandums of Understanding, >Sections for seeking new policies
- Agencies for Public dealings and Advertising,> Marketing strategies
- Personnel and their welfare, keeping ledgers of accounts.> Administrative functions

Various kinds of discrete but complexly intertwined concerns are compounded to create a proposal for a project. Slots of complex thinking can be numbered for convenience but the final compilation is a cyclical assortment of all the activities for they are equally important. Stages and phases of the development of different production units and the training of personnel for carrying out the action schemata are demarcated in the detailed plan document. Narrow casting has to be done in a locality centered purview to open micro level changes that are to be sought in civil and civic behavior. Many open-ended deliberations about forming detailed agendas, arise as suitable agents are located for setting up work forces to implement different task taking domains. The preliminary declarative exercise publicizes programs, reaches out to authorizing and financing agencies and to the persons who can enter into joint memorandums of understanding for collaborating to implement some kinds of developmental requisites. Democratic open ventures dealing with the implementing of the proposal can have small or large networks of outreach which are classified in detailed instructions about terms and conditions for preparing time bound sets of inputs to form targeted outputs.

Planned projects look into issues of training workers, laying down quality control measures and make allowances for incidental changes. Flow charts and check lists give clarity to producing knowledge as facts, features, and facets for fusing energies to build futures of growth.

- Finance and infrastructure building to house the working outreach is the base.
- Detailed lists of work and incumbents to operate different task areas are positioned in different sets of partnerships.

- Systematic work orders need frequent checks and balances.
- Eclectic mixtures of pragmatic role-playing inter relate demands with supplies, assort divisions into detailed procedures, give warnings to deal with disputed areas and uphold the perseverance that strives to deliver some benefits.
- Information about current local trends is very important in designing work schedules.
- A futuristic plan for self reliance sufficiency is included in a prepared plan document.

Organisative Model for Locality Centered Growth

Collective responsibility for recycling waste materials, voluntary guidance for uplifting the community and establishing participatory civic systems are some themes to be artfully presented.

The project proposal needs to be stated after a lot of pre preparation has been done. We make a set of slot boxes to identify the data. We divide each Slot box into structured entities such as the following :

- Information spreads state structures to perform different functions and note the provisions to manage them. Tasks and teams trained in the using of tool technologies needs specific instructions about practical work.
- Supplies of working materials, facilities for field study, tryout of practice exposure to designs and research in techniques need to be woven into the overall design.
- Title of the initiating institution that seeks joint ventures for producing products.
- Goals and objectives are stated as action taking phases and stages of formation.

- Task fields and need areas are listed as phases and stages of implementation in time and place. Norms and provisions to facilitate outreach are declared.
- Estimates of costs are projected to manage lists of pre project requirements and to cover the estimated total cost of the project as a continuing whole sphere of good growth.
- Regulations for acquiring land for making infrastructural arrangements are noted as financial outlays.
- Services by servers who perform different functions of structure are noted as numbers and costs.
- Researches, explorations, explications are to be arranged and funded.
- Major task divisions are clearly assembled. Tools, technologies, product building techniques and human power partnerships are to be configured in infrastructural terms and as financial outlays.
- Instructions and directives about regulations and skill sets are prepared.
- Action circuits and cycles are set as principles and patterns in framing techniques to deliver the goods.
- Norms about business managing systems are instituted.

Using Mass Media for Digital Governance

Large business set-ups are expansions of deals which need to announce job opportunities to select special types of work forces. On line requests for personnel seek resumes to employ experts to suit different activities.

- Makers need to know the needs of receivers and the numbers of givers who can render services.
- Financiers need to know the costs that provide the facilities

for implementing the projected task areas.

- Working partners need to clearly understand the steps and stages of joining the project.
- Facilitators need to plan the enabling of equipments and resources to the labor forces that develop objects of consumption and trading.
- Skill managers and supervisors establish the secure and safe ways of smoothly running in-house task sections.
- Aspiring teachers having different talents and skills need to be grouped to form teams to plan, prepare and process a story board for a specific teaching area. It is essential that a team of persons having different but complementary skills must come together for establishing a large objective. The overall control lies with a single authorized director.

Digital creations can be very exhausting. Free time for exercise and relaxing adventure trails have to be set aside to counterbalance high pressure media work. Awareness of Bio-rhythms is very important. We can easily get tense by being engrossed in a sophisticated digital skill and this can prevent the larger picture from coming before the limited spans of consciousness. Many examples warn us against taking the tensions of ever present conflicts too seriously. There are trans-time habits of ritual relaxation and meditation about ideals that need to be incorporated to help us in moving into complex plans that are to be translated into real time dialogues and micro time tasks.

When a partnership set is contained within a formal ritual and diurnal practice in bonds of time and work and gets positive support for progress we learn to be more responsible task takers for realizing our role-plays.

Audio-visual teaching is generally in conflict with the sponsored collages of the commercial media because thier added values do not adhere to the principles of courage, and all-round growth. Some logic of harmonious expansion has always to be incorporated in the audio-visual lesson to avoid the spread of extremist, unilateral and fascist notions.

No pictured collage of knowledge is ever isolated as selfhood is surrounded with multiple identity build ups. The organic choreography has its own legitimacy. It is better to disband a term that is not capable of bringing the outcomes and recreate a better one than to continue with an unsuccessful one.

A powerful sense of social order with glimpses of morality, ethics and refined artistry must gel together with the texts to be entered in the final copy of the computer disc. Perhaps the best practices will be picked up from the business of making good copy for advertising products but will need much more range and depth.

Chapter Seven

Courses and Practices for Digital Teaching

The digital composing of knowledge is a well designed system of outreach for applied learning that accosts some human needs and places them into systems of work for producing items of common use. New ventures are presented to revitalize, sustain, maintain and re create facilities for living within certain boundaries for blending skills and bonding together as teams of working partners. Fellow feeling is the triggering force that opens innate capacities for opening new scenarios about real time task taking to hold together our encounters with the world through our contributions.

Attributes matter the most as new skill-systems have to be acquired to build upon the unique talents persons have. Inner harmony is to be sought so that peace and good will can flourish as we work to take good care of other living beings. The eliciting of creativity in all kinds of expressions is the holistic base for getting persons to become more skillful, efficient, effective and wise in all their pursuits. While partnership goals can be logically analyzed and stated as items for instituting new ventures for shared gains the intuitive base of evolutionary growth is nebulous and works only upon personal courage which is resourced through private faith. Electronic tools of communication facilitate the instant sharing of information about strategies of human resource building in finite terms or as infinite local-to-global differences and universalities.

A digital unit is an epistemology as the "course" to be taken is the designing of applied thinking about growth as interactive endeavor. The academic foundation is merely a vast range of authentic knowledge about a theme to which different disciplines provide inputs as the definitive principles they have provided fortify programs of applied progress. The imparting of education is always a collaborative venture between thinkers and learners but the live creation of sensitizing messages depends upon bonding knowledge with the skills of expression that can be artfully and aesthetically projected.

A concept about pragmatic progress has to be developed as a complete package based upon assumptions about how to use objects through the combined talents of different workers to produce some benefits for common usage.

The initiating person has to make a comprehensive vision as well as isolate the major segments of the "turn-key" propositions for hiring different types of "services".

Preparatory research is done by locating themes of communicating through a unit by collecting data about the demands of end users who are targeted as beneficiaries. The voluntary and creative nature of participating in a venture is sought by giving added value to participants who accept allocated positions of responsibility and are accountable for preparing the sub sections of product development.

An elaborate plan document can be prepared after much research, trying out of ideas, and evolving a unit in time and place as a program of action. Different stages and phases of infrastructural needs are visualized and set in time frames of collaborative activities.

A "course design" begins by addressing a target group of policy makers who can give sanctions to get required permissions to institute work proposals. Infrastructures and provisions of materials to enable work are dealt within acquired properties within convenient places having the spaces required for carrying out work orders.

Working practices emerge from a sound knowledge of the theories from which methods for developing ideas about effective outreach can be accessed as effective and efficient modes of action. A product set is defined as component elements for which arrangements have to be made. Different areas for composite processing are identified. Detailed task analysis is undertaken to sort methodical parameters for enabling the fulfillment of work orders. Each task taking division is methodically sorted into areas which have their own distinct parameters for establishing working systems. Rules and regulations are framed to support the equities of conjoint but open participative labor.

Personnel to implement the different ranges of task taking are hired. Work forces made up of skilled persons have to be given on the job training. The task of locating different types of partners is easier now because information technologies have opened systems to collate information about who can do what for effectively collaborating to produce a need fulfilling product of consumption.

Working teams have to process different domains of product development in holistic ways for devising better futures by hiring capable persons and enrolling activists who know their communities very well, are respected by many and are highly motivated about giving their best to the cause.

Publicity has to be organized at multiple levels to share information to link the outreach of the product with the clients who can give a wide coverage for making the best use of the product. Many different arrays of contents have to be developed to frame strategies for making deals to suit the different needs of various kinds of business partners.

The internet has the ability to uplink educational resources of different kinds through specific types of research based information services. Users can freely get listed as they choose to access certain sites of information sharing. Work seekers and job creators can bond together in friendly ways to get good work accomplished.

Proposals about making changes in life styles for persons residing in large collectives depend upon up-dated research and continuous data collection as an ever present step. *Existing conditions are noted* so that better infrastructural facilities can be developed.

Types of habitats, the provision of essential supplies such as power, water, sanitation, schools, consumer goods and medical services are some important segments for data collection.

Work for wage earning is the main factor for human progress so the creation of job opportunities in locales is a major factor in helping people to help themselves. Families need the providing of homesteads, freely available food, water and electricity. Education and vocational training, communication facilities for travel and tourism and celebrating social ceremonies need special organizational attention. These and other priorities can be digitally explained so as to support and encourage public and private self governance.

A keen sensitivity about a "Whole" dominates the portions of parts which cumulatively depend upon each other in letter and spirit. The cyclic and circular collection of images as heard and felt notions is a carefully planned and edited digital model about interactive living. Digital Learning becomes a shared adventure in coping with arrays of responsibilities. Role plays are to be made very expansive and explicit in conversational ways. Special topics for search topics can be chosen to understand working relationships in families, among friends, social groups and earning opportunities. The codes, norms, forms and fashions for fusing our contributions to prevailing flows of order are ways of ratifying the bonds that bind trust to build better experiential learning.

Answers are sought for definitive questionnaires based upon the theoretic definitions of labor practices that sustain working partnerships. Guidance should be limited to general advice and confined to situated encounters for coping with various ambivalences.

Finally it is important to understand that the self guided use of the open media comes from the teacher within each of us which is to be celebrated and guarded.

The larger the scope of the communicative project the greater is the care needed to include different kinds of environments for working in harmony. Guidance and counseling is to be provided at every stage so that conflicts of interests can be dealt with and partnerships can maintain a well knit shape and form. While monetary incentives are significant factors critical appreciation and support for innovating creative visions has long lasting internalized value and therefore a lot of seed money is essential to provide this root force.

A cross-section of persons coming within a common category have to be contacted, interviewed and encouraged to talk about the real issues that matter in the partnerships they are held accountable for. Humane humanism patiently deals with persons who hold different positions and stay within some parameters of order. The strife that reinvents our value syndromes is set in situated encounters to critically mirror the underlying validations that people hold. Alternate approaches and better propositions are presented to open new options that are made evident and decorated enough to make strong appeals. Factors that affect the processing of partnerships are addressed in simple, entertaining and easy-to-accept ways. Sincerity about taking responsibility is as important as the modes and methods of performing tasks to excel. A variety program approach removes some confusion about role-persona attitudes to make space for some new searches.

A guide needs to be very sure about how much information can be accepted in what kinds of ways in a time and effort based situated encounter. Teachers need to keep improving upon their skills to seek higher levels of creative competence. There is a very powerful mystically Divine Super-Rhythm that enters into our consciousness when we whole-heartedly believe in the immediate, short and long term value of what we communicate.

Optional Areas to Develop Practical Skill Sets

Formal Training in the Multi-Languages that are Used to Compose Concepts

Story boards are prepared by linking clips of texts, visuals and recordings to compose slots of inclusive understanding. Studies and practices dealing with the structural, literary and ethno-linguistic patterns are made to share holistic perceptions about life living. Models about using techniques for artistically operating through various electronic tools are to be shared so that new sights can be set for improving acquired competence.

Working on assignments by being attached to professional business ventures is a preparatory exercise that has to be undertaken to get the confidence in applying concepts.

Formal Training in Fine Arts

Developing competence in sketching and painting to design contents in colorful ways and being familiar with lighting, sound effects and backdrop framing gives the setting to the scenario within which live meaningful understanding is established.

Learning to illustrate text messages, make posters, form tags to differentiate sections being posted, use decorative outlines and different fonts to note different facts, distinguish factors through comments and make notes about different features are very important preparatory exercises.

Formal Training in Performing Arts

Sound effects and musical expertise in instrumental and sung styles are specialized talents for enhancing impacts by establishing suitable emotion centered moods.

Formal Training in Communication Styles and Arts

Dialogues and debates, giving commentaries about events, gathering articles about happenings, using dialects and idioms to hold and sustain interest, using anecdotes and gathering clips from different sources, developing story lines, devising strategies for interviewing in humane ways, making a series on developmental and other civic policy based issues and commenting to build correct and desirable opinions, managing talk shows and giving counsel, adjusting with feedbacks and enabling healthy growth in diverse ways.

Formal Training in Data Collection

Understanding how to record events, hold interviews, tap

resources from different libraries and using voice recorders, photographs and movie cameras to gather information. Client centered data analysis is an important exercise in extracting only what is required.

Professional teachers need to build portfolios and collages to display their efficiency and to prepare job profiles. It is easier to sequence story lines when the basic points are available when a widespread sociolinguistic coverage of an area/locale/segment is prepared. An objective distance is a personal control that has to be exercised to prevent getting over involved in the problems of others or even ones own ambitions.

Skill Sets for Framing Dialogue Sessions

An agenda is formed by breaking a set of problems into democratic open participative discussions. Salient features about proposals are presented.

There are five major divisions for initiating dialogues; the content ranges, the work practices, the fixed assets, the hardware needs and the technical expertise for preparing units. Different components have a site based situation building framework that is noted and organized. Circuits of supplies and demands are presented as configured estimates and provisions are made as aggregates for production. Key questions are raised to tackle difficult issues. Free association is interspersed with the aim of the deliberation. The emotional over-reacting to, or under-playing a role-set to be taken is accepted but has to be controlled by the chairperson. Brainstorming opens new possibilities. Group discussions give a sense of belonging to sustain the quantity and the quality of a venture. The personality cult gives way to fusions of opinions and strategies are accepted by consensus.

Report writing is essential so that summaries can be made and follow up actions can be taken. Leadership by one is essential but dealings are set into slot based positions for managing relevant areas and sections that are woven together to provide serviceable products.

Structuring Messages to Frame Learning Sessions

The scope and range of the project has to be established by defining details for all tentative participating partners. An agenda is framed by breaking a set of problems into slots for finding some solutions. Contours are laid out as aggregates to work upon salient features. Supply and demand circuits are explained as specifications and provisions. Lead questions are framed and randomly used to elicit true answers and work for some consensus about coping with some issues about accepting new paths as tasks. Free association is interspersed with deliberated aims to get better strategies in encounters. Overreacting and underplaying are emotional dramas that need subtle and delicate conversational competence. Self assessment comes easily when dialogues pinpoint routine responses by making brief tag questions rather than comments.

Negotiating for a better deal becomes the key factor in getting commitments to improve static or negative blocks in relationships.

Fields of discourse conversationally open models that can be tried out to satisfy different needs of different customers. Spot questions that need quick answers are prepared to elicit hidden truths.

Pre-production dialogue is scattered but gradually consensus emerges to prepare final expositions. It is necessary to put in place some essential consultative costs, frame realistic targets for developing rapport in work spaces and manage client centered expectations. Getting advice from local thinkers and participating in ceremonies provides the face to face informality that emotionally connects teams. Friendly fellowship is the core factor that takes people away from the humdrum of daily hard work and opens new perceptions. Field work to establish on site sensitization is as important as the technical aspects that develop a product.

Some Techniques for Staging Useful Dialogues

- Frankly talking about contradictory positions and casually noting antithetical attitudes and uninformed hastily made stances.
- Looking deeper into the uses and misuses of emotions such as anger, over affection, aversion, admiration, over assertiveness, rigidity and so on.
- Challenging opinions framed as negative terms by confronting persons with their habitual weaknesses.
- Using odd game ploys to get to the heart of a matter on hand.
- Anchors always need to be fair and just towards all the suggestions shared in the discussion event.
- Open requests are gathered and answered immediately or within the next meeting.
- Self help group activities for spreading welfare needs among disadvantaged persons is encouraged and given support in a discussion group.

Skill Building in Using Technological Tools

This compulsory field needs advice from experts along with slow, gradual and patient work schedules. In a general way one can offer some guidance but the main task of undertaking exercises for mixing and merging texts with graphic designs and art forms to suit the objectives of an operational design for interaction is a performance that needs careful handling. Choreographing a digital learning module entails the following:

- We identify dramatic techniques to place content matters into impact making experiences,
- We respect all efforts to attain competence in textual clarity and brevity,
- We can opt to acquire expertise in photography, cinematography and editing or script preparation,
- We gain expertise using computer aided software to design story boards as artwork,
- We learn to use computer tools to animate modules as steps and stages of formation,
- We try to show what is possible in probabilistic frameworks
- We use many real life instances to give veracity to the model we create.

A Checklist for Constructing a Digital Unit

- A digital encapsulation is a business which reaches out to the public like any other dealing in the commercial sector.
- A vision about a project begins with a title. A preamble gives the gist of the overall plan as it defines objectives.
- Development of resources to build some type of consumable products is listed and categorized as joint partnerships to manage diverse types of duties.
- The high costs of production are formulated in detail. The place of work, salaries for workers, cost of equipments, providing tools, organizing suitable intellectual inputs and

counting overhead costs and incidental expenses is a specialized management exercise that has to be undertaken. Use of Hardware to develop software is a slow and time consuming skill building exploration which needs eclectic guidance from many technical and creative experts. Seminars and workshops are required for motivating persons to open new ways of thinking.

- Sophisticated possibilities in using visual images and sound effects are essential for motivating persons in realizing the delicate art of co-operating in committed ways.
- Plans have to be discussed as domains to form complete sub-constructs that are separately undertaken by different members of action teams. Confusions need to be rectified and complicated issues are opened for voluntary contributions by the receivers of messages. Any contradictory elements are removed to retain the positive experience that leads to growth.
- Role plays are made productive by adhering to the functions to be displayed in the final product. Duties for each participant are stated in definitive ways. The following elements have to be adhered to; Function and use, method of production, technique and design, time and effort of labor and its cost, personal skills and ingenuity of expressing ourselves and the combining of the exchanges to create a viable unit.
- Pre-training to get the right kinds of trainee candidates is an expensive exercise. Questionnaires and data gathering sheets of different kinds are prepared to simplify the elaborate procedures that are devised by a team of specialists. Holding interviews, taking photographs, filming live incidents are some modes to be subsequently fused into a holistic unit.

- Domains for collective effort are sorted into slots which are further segmented as differentiated codes. An area of concern is mapped into captions that are accumulated as contents which finally come together after much try out and editing.
- Sentence patterns are brief but they pack together complex ranges in compounded dimensions for saying what we want to share in different situations. Divisions become domains that are defined for producing the goods to be shared
- Design is a rhythmic use of techniques that focus upon different strategies for making memorable impacts.
- Time and effort of labor has a cost element that is gauged according to portfolios about skills as in ingenious ways of expressing contents.
- Gains and losses are measured and balanced to establish longer lasting securities.
- Public relations and the marketing of the prepared product is a shared activity undertaken by all members of work teams.
- In the periodic and final reports the collaborators are listed along with the contributions they have made.
- Publicity materials and training programs are devised to ensure self sufficiency after the initial expenditure is met. Detailed plans and programs of production are attached as attachments or are separately supplied to interested parties.
- Freedom to use traditional cultural artifacts to enhance a chosen style derived from a conventional genre is accepted. Equally valid is a new approach to a familiar tradition.
- In the work sphere responsibilities are immense and get multiplied as the presence of deadlines for completing jobs further add to the take over the time bound nature of the activity sets.

School Level Courses for Digital Thinking

Starting from pre-school levels, the non-controversial ways of mutually shared thinking has to be woven into educational units. The exposition of knowledge as travels in space and time provides the impetus to venture far into new areas of creativity. Non controversial approaches to different relationships in friendly and honest ways pave the way for co-operating to get what one wants. Moral values have to be lived out by trainers before one can hope to transfer them to children. Interfaith experiences are needed to show the differences that color the unity in the world. The shift to the play-way mode has to be innovatively utilized to share situation based information. Skill building should be team based so that sharing can be inculcated in enthusiastic play-way modes. Clubs for photography and filming need to be supported. Field visits and theatrical activities are incorporated. Original designs for scriptwriting are formulated. Making scrap books, story telling, theatre and drama competitions, debates and descriptions of travels are some popular methods for developing digital lessons. Computer aided poster making to create special purpose class displays such as news-sheets and mini magazines lay a strong foundation for elaborate uses in later life.

Small projects need to be devised as exercises for skill building. Vocabulary can be made inclusive to list sets of objectives that are topic based or closely associated as adverbial connectives for adding on possible options about meaningful interacting. Audio-visual communicating is very topical and touches upon all kinds of contemporary issues. Vocational studies have become so important that they need to be identified from childhood itself. The problems of adolescence need to be dealt with great sensitivity which participative talk shows can do very effectively.

Professional Digital Communication

A project proposal leads to a greater awareness about how different participators become benefactors in order to become beneficiaries. Larger projects need to string many layers of thought to show how benefits can be created to serve the needs of primary developers, secondary work teams and tertiary beneficiaries through specific types of task taking.

An Audio-visual unit sets a goal for itself, notes the importance of its objectives, presents the aims of its tasks and gives alternatives about competence for striving to attain a set of functional purposes. The lesson a picture can drive home is worth many oral explanations. The warmth of a rich and deep voice ordains great value to a message and is highly prized in the audio-visual media.

Commentators bind diversity by repeating key features in a democratically open opinion gathering structured dialogue. They have the added responsibility for reducing chaos and strengthening socially oriented attitudes in controlling wild fancies.

Descriptions about the shape and size of products need the additional references to sets of expectations along with clarifying the objectives. Instructions need to be set as notices that also expose belts of stages in cyclically phased wholes of fabrication. Open information about different factors such as costs, recurring expenditures, types and quantities of work orders, and as up/down access and information modalities make action packages collectively democratic.

While practical logical information can easily be contained in a unit, the inner, deeper empowerment is much harder to manage. How do private concerns impact the written, spoken, felt and projected signs of public presences? How do conventions affect our understanding of self realization? How does habit affect the openness that brings about potentials for growth? How does trust strengthen will power? How does example teach us to make new beginnings? There are no answers to many of our questions but there are intuitive thoughts that come from experience, from sincere selfless thinking and from the wisdom of the ages that offers some peaceful consolations. All these questions need subtle explication, aesthetic exposition, and open ended inclusion to help us in being realistic about situations and knowledge frames.

Self control is a core foundation of character building that has to be understood, explained, explored, invoked, reinforced, sustained and shared in all possible ways. Loyalty and careful caring, humility in sharing creative energy and the courage to effectively implement a planned concept are some other very human traits that need to become story lines.

The self sacrificing super ego needs the strength that a personally ratified Dharma ordains. Religion needs to be acknowledged as an empowering essence that supports situation centered controls to handle unavoidable contradictions. Innovative suggestions for establishing effective support systems arise from a strong faith as well as a detached but dedicated approach to a love for enthusiastically striving to constantly nurture life. Dissipative tendencies need the blessing of prayer that showers peaceful rays of contentment upon our spiritual self disciplines.

Teachers have to choose how to become competent in specific vocational fields in order to give the right advice to students.

Internet facilities such as portals having many networks aid. Professional audio-visual training teachers should forecast demand and supply chains to satisfy the ever expanding knowledge environments to understand contemporary clashes of values.

Audio-visual teachers need to counsel students about the professional areas that would suit the skills they possess. Tensions about careers no longer have to be restricted to safety nets derived from parental or family traditions. The global presence of job seeking is a research area in itself for locating the right opportunities to learn and earn. The onus of growth lies in the political domain as infrastructural needs have to be met but unless the new patterns of dynamic advocacy are explored and exposed by teachers themselves this cannot happen. Proposals need to be made where different kinds of requirements and learning inputs have to be clearly listed as well as defined to get the outputs that can enhance the sense of self worth populaces in our local-to-global-to-local world. It is very important to go along with regional and national cultural conditionings to manage the challenges of growth to be dealt with by very temperamental human partners. Ethnic arts have an aesthetic base that peacefully produces attractive gifts for sharing by tribal communities. The commercial value given to village handicrafts needs to maintain a peaceful approach that does not clash with the routine lifestyles of the inhabitants.

Digital band-spreads of cohesive understanding are very good guides to initiate innovative action but the face to face interaction is essential when the parties concerned discuss matters. The basic teaching needs to be steered by wise counseling and efficiently monitored feed backs. Life cycle strategies for grassroots implementation of all projects about all round growth need the energy that a news reporter has. A special interest perspective has to submit to the general interest of all those who will be concerned/affected by transnational ventures.

Combinations of Disciplines for Higher Learning

There are three Major Segments of Study and Action Research. A the Theory Group, B the Ground Area, C Practice and Skills

Language and Literature

Social linguistics, Media scripting, Performing arts, Community theatre, Journalism, Applied Sociology, Creative writing, Advertising skills, Fine arts and Graphic design.

Sociology

Culture studies, Ethno-linguistics, Cross cultures, Urban or rural patterns, Folk traditions, Sectors of media practices, Religious beliefs, Social mediation, Family interactions and Surveys and services.

Economics

Financial security, Wage & work balances, Markets & trade, Services & structures, Home economics, Equities and resources, Commercial exchanging of Consumer goods, Business services and Provisions and productivity.

Stage Arts

Settings Lighting, Decor and script needs, Pictorial features, Photo arts and Filming techniques, forms and genres, Classical and folk traditions, Sketching the script techniques and tool technologies, Special effects and speech matching with visuals, Editing and mixing sequences with sound bytes, Continuity in splicing film cuts for even flows.

Philosophical Traditions

Classical Indian with Regional inputs, Western/eastern forms and Conventions, Design features and Aesthetics, Styles and sensation building poetics, Normative Texts, Regulations for establishing practices and culturally cohesive world views.

Environment Care
Heritages, Documentaries of resource sites, Natures gifts Preservation and Regeneration, Health and hygiene, Rites and ritual necessities.

History
Civilization, Readings of facts and features, Current affairs, Reporting and recorded events, Contemporary matters, Sifting out newsworthiness from large volumes of information.

Applied Sciences
Products and usages, Systems of production.

Electronics
Technologies and tools, Usages and User competence.

Law and Jurisprudence
Civil rules and multi level self governance.

Architecture
Habitats and harmony in provided spaces for growth.

Languages
Special purpose dialects and site based veracity.

There can be many diverse combinations of segments and sub-sections that can be devised and presented by teachers.

Organizing Multi Skills for Developing Expertize

- Communication studies and practices are networks that bring together persons having special skills and so it is necessary to develop data banks and have display files to get team work in place.
- Special competence is needed to create story boards with clips of texts and graphic figures. Episodes can be clips of

filmed reality or simulated representations of reality. Editing skills to incorporate sound bytes and conversations into texts is another complex area requiring very detailed practical work.

- A route map for following some nation wide and international establishments educates persons in human resources management. Integrated development in economic, social, political, psychological and emotional dimensions of real existence has to be pursued. This helps in ascertaining clear cut positions about exploring the professional researches that build holistic project proposals.
- Research work in holistic approaches to role arrays, locality management, civic services for different urban or rural areas, land usages and distribution for industrial and technological purposes, production cycles and equitable distribution of produced goods, integrated economics and recycling of finances, special education for disabled persons are some directions for exploring holistic communication.
- Integrating communicative choices with aptitudes is a personal domain for developing fields of interaction in preparation for professional undertakings.
- Learning to fuse different types of theoretical concepts in multi-logical patterns to nurture the ambits, ambiences and ambivalences has to be covered in project proposal.
- How to enable participative interaction in managing outlays with essential provisions indicates how to get suitable servers. Building togetherness by creating rapport and sharing aspirations is essential. Holding discussion sessions to talk about controversial issues, common problems and operational system is essential. Some themes are; livelihoods and sets of demand/supply chains, habitats and

markets for exchanging survival needs, state policies and local politics for distributing resources to serve people.

- Studying human rights as responsibilities is a core area. Skills and systems about using applied arts in serving the interests of different kinds of benefactors and beneficiaries is the practice. Establishing team worked systems to produce goods and looking after training needs and welfare activities is the enabling factor.
- Acquiring information about governance and state laws to plan joint ventures as action patterns is a preparatory base.

In conclusion the transit from lateral and linear thinking to cyclic and circular perception management is a complete make over in designing systems for imparting teacher training. There are no limits to growth but each one of us has great expertise in some way of communicating our strongly felt convictions which has to be rounded off in very sociological terms. The free market forces in our globally connected world are very competitive; so the desire to excel on the basis of some solid foundations is the greatest gift a teacher can acquire and pass on to others.

Selected Bibliographic References

The Bhagwata Gita and the *Isha, Mandukya, Taittireya* and *Chhandogya Upanishads* provide many pragmatic insights towards envisaging wise growth.

Gautama Buddha sees the mind as the principle of individuation, manifestation, transformation, succession and discrimination which is to be considered by meditating on compassion, the struggle for purity, and the search for likeness, rhythm, harmony, permanence and peace.

Sri Shankaracharya explicates Vedanta. A small text, Pancikaranam, Advaita Ashrama, Ramakrishna Mission, Calcutta establishes a system for perceiving reality in a holistic format that blends the five elements into diverse forms of being.

Plato and many other Greek and Roman thinkers laid the foundations for the dialectics that condition human dialogue.

St Augustine, City of God, views the Soul in the body as a Whole and in each part thereof. Human history is a progressive movement that is redeemed by God.

The growth of Human Studies was a powerful movement in Europe *Immanual Kant,* Berkeley, Hume, Schopenhauer, Spinoza And Pascal have been some of the major thinkers laying a tradition for showing how Humanism rests upon the search for the spirit within the self.

Critical studies made by *Nietzsche, Hegel, Heidigger, Husserl* culminated in conceptual theories such as Phenomenology and Structuralism.

Studies in psychological impacts, (Freud and Jung), linguistic semantics as sociological determination, (Wittgenstein and Saussure), kinship patterns of anthropology and myths, (Levi Strauss), open education and its free selectivity, (Piaget), were some leading patterns of exploring the world as the Hermeneutics of perception.

Wilhem Dilthey pioneered Human Studies by explaining phenomenology as Ethnomethodology. The work of social scientists such as *Weber, Gadamer, Habermas, Schutz, Erikson, Horkheimer,* paved the way for the rise of the empirical practices that have now culminated as life organizing Management Studies.

G A Kelly, The psychology of personal constructs, Norton N Y 1955, explains the forming of core roles and their conserves to play out applied humanism.

Merleu Ponty, The phenomenology of perception, Routledge and Kegan Paul, London, 1962, clearly stated that science must see itself as a construction based on a brute, existent world.

Kenneth Burke, A grammar of motives in society, ed. Hugh Duncan, Oxford Univ Press, 1968 is a very significant contribution.

B F Skinner, Beyond freedom and dignity, A A Knopf 1971 extols the new wave philosophy of the sanctity of the role.

T A Mcarthy, A theory of Communication; Philosophy of the Social Sciences, vol. 3 1973 opens practices for directing interaction to manage the media.

Francis S Collins. The language of god. Free Press 2006 moots the concept of bio-logos as a harmony of science and faith to locate the moral law of selecting the right path to love life.

The work of path finding thinkers such as *J L Austin* in How to do things with word opened scholarship areas on the syntactical impacts of the sociology of language.

Raymond Williams, Keywords, Fontana, London, 1983 brilliantly explored the power of language as thought.

M Mcluhan, Understanding media, the extension of man, Mcgraw Hill, N Y 1964 is considered a prophet for the evolution of Mass Communication.

Eli Ginzberg, The manpower connection ; Education and Work, Harvard Univ Press 1975 establishes the specialization of information for the labor forces.

Edward De Bono. Monographs on Lateral Thinking, Six Thinking Hats, Six Action Shoes and The Happiness Purpose, Penguin, 1979 humorously suggests ways of dealing with multi-leveled thinking.

A J Croply, Towards a system of lifelong education, 1980, UNESCO Institute for Education, Hamburg, outlines many practical approaches.

Frithof Capra, The Turning Point : Science, Society and the Rising Culture, Wildwood House, London, 1982 is a guide to holistic education.

Howard Gardner. Multiple intelligence theory ; Web of Life, Harper Collins is perhaps the most lucid explication regarding information management.

Raimondo Pannikkar, Myth, Faith and Hermeneutics, 1983

Media Studies in Education, UNESCO Report 1980. and Learning to Care, Education for the Twenty-first Century, UNESCO Report, 1990, are definitive studies.

D V K Murthy. studies in indian aesthetics and criticism, Mysore 1979. *D K Ghosh,* ed, Digital India, UBSPB, 2006. *Tony* and *Barry Buzan,* The Mind Map book, BBC Books, 1993 is the most effective tool for constructing the deliberative and the routinely prepared ranges of understanding diversity.

BOSTI Buffalo Organisation for Social and Technological Innovation, 812 Kenmore Avenue New York

Steven Anzalone. Multi Channel Learning, Washington and

Ken Wilbur, The Eye of the Spirit, Sambhala, Boston and London, 1990, clearly depicts the integrative phenomenology of all human knowledge that meditatively deconstructs by re-evaluating stances to be taken.

R K Mookerji, Ancient Indian Education; Brahminical and Buddhist, Motilal Benarasidas, 1969 is a good reference work.

It is important to know about ancient Classical studies such as Natyashastra, the Rasa theory, the concept of Sadharanikarana and Shastram Kavya on the aesthetic of combining various performing arts to enrich knowledge framing in audio-visual formats.

Sri Aurobindo, The volume of collected discourses, The Human Cycle published by Sri Aurobindo Ashram 1977 presents the complexity of self awareness for understanding evolutionary growth

Sirkka Minkkinen, A general Curricular Model for Mass media education, UNESCO sponsored project, by E S C O, Spain, gives an overall scenario for organizing curricular patterns.

Marmar Mukhopadhyay, ed. Education for a Global Society, Shipra Publications, India, 2003, sponsored by The Temple of Understanding lists multifaith dimensions of value building.

Rajni Tandon, Applied Humanities; Integrated Curricular Structures for Developmental Communication, Sterling, India 1989 offers a non-formal approach to formal knowledge designs.

Values for Audio-visual Learning, Shipra Publications, 2004 is a web-paged book about inclusive thinking.